SPANISH
FOR TOURISTS

The Most Essential Spanish Guide to Travel Abroad, Meet People & Find Your Way Around - *All While Speaking Perfect Spanish!*

By Dagny Taggart

Disclaimer

The information provided in this book is designed to provide helpful information on the subjects discussed. The author's books are only meant to provide the reader with the basics knowledge of a certain language, without any warranties regarding whether the student will, or will not, be able to incorporate and apply all the information provided. Although the writer will make her best effort share her insights, language learning is a difficult task, and each person needs a different timeframe to fully incorporate a new language. This book, nor any of the author's books constitute a promise that the reader will learn a certain language within a certain timeframe.

Table of Contents

MY FREE GIFT TO YOU! 9

>> GET THE FULL SPANISH ONLINE COURSE WITH AUDIO LESSONS <<...............**10**

INTRODUCTION: PREPARE YOURSELF, WE'RE ABOUT TO DEPART! 11

    BUILDING A FOUNDATION IN SPANISH.. 11

    CULTURALLY SPEAKING 12

    THE 'MAÑANA' CONCEPT 12

    HONESTY IS THE BEST POLICY 13

    THE MELTING POT OF LATIN AMERICA 13

    YEAH! ANOTHER RELIGIOUS HOLIDAY! 13

    GESTICULAR DIFFERENTIATION.. 14

    LEARNING TO LIVE IN LACK OF LUXURY 14

CHAPTER 1: BASIC PRONUNCIATION GUIDELINES...................................**15**

    VOWEL PRONUNCIATION CHART 15

    CONSONANT PRONUNCIATION CHART 15

    GRAMMAR 17

    PARTS OF SPEECH 18

    QUESTION WORDS 30

    MOST COMMONLY USED WORDS 30

    PHRASES TO USE WHEN CONFUSED 31

    FRIENDLY PHRASES 31

    EXCLAMATIONS 32

    TIME EXPRESSIONS 32

    MORE RANDOM, USEFUL PHRASES 33

    COLORS 33

    NUMBERS 1-10 33

    NUMBERS 11-20 34

    NUMBERS 30-100+ 34

    NUMBERS 200-1000 35

CHAPTER 2: TRAVELLING, LODGING & HOW TO FIND YOUR WAY AROUND........**36**

    AIRPORT PHRASES 36

    PUBLIC TRANSPORTATION 39

    TAKING TAXIS 39

Buses, Trains, and Subways oh my! 39

Finding Accommodation 43

Hotel Vocabulary 43

Hotel Meals 43

Hotel Ammenities 43

¿Qué necesitas? (What do you need?) 44

Wandering Around 46

¿Dónde está? (Where is it?) 47

Lugares (Places) 47

Otras frases (Other phrases) 48

CHAPTER 3: CRASH GUIDE TO SOCIAL SKILLS IN SPANISH **51**

Meet and greet *51*

Saludando (Saying Hi) 51

¿Cómo les va? (How are you all doing?) 52

Parting is such sweet sorrow 52

Cuénteme más de ti (Tell me more about yourself) 52

Describing your world 55

Phrases to describe each other 55

More Description Phrases and Vocabulary 56

How ya feeling? 58

Phrases using 'Tener' 60

Expressions using 'Tener' 60

Occupations 63

Career Vocabulary 63

Family Matters 68

Phrases to talk about your immediate Family 69

Phrases to talk about Extended Family 70

Bonus: Think about how you would describe your family in Spanish. 73

CHAPTER 4: HAVING FUN IN THE CITY (SHOPPING, DINING, NIGHTLIFE) **74**

Shopping Around 74

¿Dónde y cómo ir de compras? (Where and how to shop) 74

Más frases de compras (More shopping phrases) 75

La Ropa de Damas (Women's Clothing) 76

La Ropa de Caballeros (Men's Clothing) 76

La Ropa de Invierno (Winter Clothing) 77

La Ropa de Verano (Summer Clothing) 77

Compras para la Casa (Shopping for the home) 78

Bonus: Size Conversion Chart 80

Women's Clothing Sizes 80

Women's Shoe Sizes 80

Men's Clothing Sizes 81

Men's Shoe Sizes 81

Children's Clothing Sizes 81

Wining and Dining 81

Reservando una Mesa (Reserving a Table) 82

(Pidiendo la comida) Ordering 82

Food preferences 84

More Food Vocabulary 84

Nightlife phrases 87

Let's ... (Vamos a...) 87

Vamos a tomar un trago (Let's have a drink) 88

Dating Scene 90

¡El Rechazo! (Rejection!) 91

Cultural Visits and Activities 93

Me gustaría ir ... (I would like to go...) 93

Perdón, quisiera (Excuse me, I would like...) 93

Necesito información. (I need some information.) 94

Sports and Outdoors.. 95

Los Deportes (Sports) 96

Ven conmigo a ...(Come with me to...) 96

Quisiera ir (I would like to go...) 97

CHAPTER 5: "HELP ME OUT, PLEASE!" 100

Necesito... (I need...) 100

Enfermedades leves (Minor ailments)... 101

Partes del cuerpo (Body parts).. 101

Más frases (More phrases) 102

Emergencias (Emergencies) 104

Ayúdeme (Help me!)... 105

Necesito... (I need...) 105

Money in the Bank 107

Banking Phrases... 107

Hay un problema... (There is a problem...) 108

Time will tell 110

¿QUÉ HORA ES? (WHAT TIME IS IT?)...110

¿QUÉ DÍA ES HOY? (WHAT DAY IS TODAY?) 111

¿CUÁL ES LA FECHA HOY? (WHAT IS THE DATE TODAY?) 111

¿QUÉ TIEMPO HACE HOY? (WHAT IS THE WEATHER LIKE TODAY)......115

How's the Weather? Answers 117

CHAPTER 6: EXTRA MATERIAL YOU'LL DEFINITELY USE DOWN THE ROAD........ 118

EL SUPERMERCADO (SUPERMARKET) 118

BUSCO... (I AM LOOKING FOR...) 119

LA SALUD Y LA 120

ARTÍCULOS DE BELLEZA (BEAUTY ITEMS) 120

PELUQUERÍA (HAIR SALON) 122

CORTES DE PELO (HAIRCUTS) 122

CUIDADO, TENGO... (CAREFUL, I HAVE...) 123

THE WORLD WIDE WEB 125

VOCABULARIO DEL COMPUTADOR (COMPUTER VOCABULARY) 125

POR FAVOR, ME AYUDA, NECESITO... (PLEASE, HELP ME, I NEED...).................125

NAVEGANDO POR EL INTERNET 126

AYÚDAME, NECESITO... (HELP ME, I NEED TO...) 126

CHAPTER 7: THE TOP TEN, MOST BEAUTIFUL PLACES TO VISIT IN SPAIN 130

TOP TEN PLACES TO VISIT IN SPAIN 130

1. BARCELONA 130

2. MADRID 130

3. SEVILLE 130

4. VALENCIA 131

5. BILBAO 131

6. GRANADA 131

7. CORDOBA 131

8. TOLEDO 131

9. SALAMANCA 132

10. SANTIAGO DE COMPOSTELA 132

BONUS CITY! 132

BUNOL 132

COMMON SLANG USED IN SPAIN 132

GREAT LANGUAGE-LEARNING WEBSITES 134

CONCLUSION: ARE YOU READY? YOUR JOURNEY BEGINS NOW! 138

>> GET THE FULL SPANISH ONLINE COURSE WITH AUDIO LESSONS << 139

PS: CAN I ASK YOU A QUICK FAVOR? 140

PREVIEW OF "LEARN SPANISH IN 7 DAYS! - THE ULTIMATE CRASH COURSE TO LEARN THE BASICS OF THE SPANISH LANGUAGE IN NO TIME" 141

CHECK OUT MY OTHER BOOKS..148

ABOUT THE AUTHOR... 149

Dedicated to those who love going beyond their own frontiers.

Keep on traveling,

Dagny Taggart

My FREE Gift to You!

As a way of saying thank you for downloading my book, I'd like to send you an exclusive gift that will revolutionize the way you learn new languages. It's an extremely comprehensive PDF with 15 language hacking rules that **will help you learn 300% <u>faster</u>, with <u>less effort</u>, and with <u>higher than ever retention rates</u>**.

This guide is an amazing complement to the book you just got, and could easily be a stand-alone product, but for now I've decided to give it away for free, to thank you for being such an awesome reader, and to make sure I give you all the value that I can to help you succeed faster on your language learning journey.

To get your FREE gift, follow the link below, write down your email address and I'll send it right away!

>> http://bit.ly/SpanishGift <<

GET **INSTANT** ACCESS

>> Get The Full Spanish Online Course With Audio Lessons <<

If you truly want to learn Spanish 300% FASTER, then hear this out.

I've partnered with the most revolutionary language teachers to bring you the very best Spanish online course I've ever seen. It's a mind-blowing program specifically created for language hackers such as ourselves. It will allow you learn Spanish 3x faster, straight from the comfort of your own home, office, or wherever you may be. It's like having an unfair advantage!

The Online Course consists of:

+ 185 Built-In Lessons
+ 98 Interactive Audio Lessons
+ 24/7 Support to Keep You Going

The program is extremely engaging, fun, and easy-going. You won't even notice you are learning a complex foreign language from scratch. And before you realize it, by the time you go through all the lessons you will officially become a truly solid Spanish speaker.

Old classrooms are a thing of the past. It's time for a language revolution.

If you'd like to go the extra mile, follow the link below and let the revolution begin

>> http://www.bitly.com/Spanish-Course <<

CHECK OUT THE COURSE »

Introduction
Prepare Yourself, We're About to Depart!

To truly learn a language one must commit to hours of studying and in the best scenario travel to the country where that language is spoken. However, what if you want to just prepare to go to that country in order to survive and get by with what you need? This book is the survival guide just for this purpose! It is set up in a simple way so that you can quickly find what you need specific to your situation. We will offer language that covers topics including travel, business, everyday life, social events, meeting new people, and introducing yourself to name a few. Each chapter will provide examples and opportunities to practice and test the knowledge that you have obtained. After each section, there are practice questions and the answers immediately follow them. So don't worry if you get stuck on one. Just try your best, use context clues if you don't know a word, then check the answer. You will notice some vocabulary and phrases are repeated throughout the book. Language repetition is key in retaining new vocabulary!

When you finish with this book you will be ready to travel and enjoy the Spanish-speaking country of your choice. We also include a bonus at the end of the book recommending ten of the best places to visit along with some useful slang to help you sound like a native in Spain (or at least like a very knowledgeable gringa or gringo.) Along with this, we offer several language learning web sites to further your language development. Remember to have an open mind and realize that languages do not translate word for word but rather through ideas. Also, don't worry about making mistakes in the language because they just provide opportunities for you to learn more! Remember to have fun and you will have a wonderful language learning journey. Let's get started!

Building a Foundation in Spanish

The introduction will give you a general description of Spanish-speaking culture, pronunciation, grammatical structure, and lastly provide you with useful words and phrases in Spanish. Understanding culture is such an important part of being able to communicate with others. Language is definitely more than just verbal. Facial expressions, gestures, body language, etc. all contribute to communication. Along with this we will give you a base for pronunciation and grammatical structure. Correct pronunciation is essential to language learning. Some letters in Spanish are pronounced in a very different way than in English. I will provide you with a pronunciation guide for this. You also can use many of the language websites we suggest at the end of the book or google translate to help you pronounce the words in Spanish. Lastly, understanding the order and structure of the language is necessary to make sure you are communicating clearly. Using these three topics, this chapter will give you a base to get started learning the Spanish language!

Culturally Speaking

Every Spanish-speaking country has a slightly different culture but there are some similarities that you will find throughout. A common thread I have found throughout Latin America is the hospitality. If you go to someone's home they are most likely going to offer you something to drink, eat, and maybe even give you some fruit or vegetables to take home. You feel incredibly welcome, like you are in your own home. The importance of family and closeness of friends and neighbors is another common characteristic. I find in American culture individual achievement is most important. In contrast, in Latin-American cultures helping each other, whether it be family, friends or neighbors, is priority. You sometimes will find that within a neighborhood, the neighbors live as if they were family, in and out of each other's houses, in constant contact with each other. Our culture of being holed up in our home and having minimum contact with neighbors is unheard of. Below are the categories of culture that we will discuss.

> *-The 'Mañana' Concept*
> *-Honesty is the Best Policy*
> *-The Melting Pot of Latin America*
> *-Yeah! Another religious Holiday!*
> *-Gesticular Differentiation*
> *-Learning to Live in Lack of Luxury*

The 'Mañana' Concept

You will also find that the Latin American concept of time is quite different. The culture is generally more relaxed than ours when it comes to time. When it comes to services in almost any realm, you will have to be reminded that patience is a virtue. If a party is scheduled at 7pm, you might be expected to show up at 9. If a company is scheduled to install the internet in your apartment on Thursday at 3pm, you can expect them the following Wednesday around 6pm. In many countries, it is also true that businesses will close down in the afternoon from two to four hours for lunch. People also have a long lunch hour and will go home to *'almorzar'* (to eat lunch) and take a nap before going back to work. These usually means they will end up getting off work around 7 or 8 instead of 5.

Honesty is the Best Policy

Along with this, you will notice that honesty truly is the best policy in most Latin-American cultures. So don't feel bad if someone tells you it seems that you are a little more **gordito** (chubby) since the last time they saw you or if your hair just seems incredibly dry and you need a deep conditioning treatment. I believe their opinion is that they are helping out the other person by commenting on their flaws so he or she can become a better person. Just take it with a grain of salt, nod, and smile. I think it is always helpful to be prepared for these kinds of moments so that you do not get offended by the other party. It is common for everyone to be involved in each other's lives and try to help the other even if you don't feel like you need it. Again don't take offense, smile, and move on.

The Melting Pot of Latin America

The majority of Spanish-speaking countries are countries that have been colonized and **conquistado** (conquered) by another country (Spain). This typically means that these countries include a plethora of people: the Indigenous people of the country, Europeans, and Africans. This results in a culture that draws from many different backgrounds. Catholicism is the most common religion that often will have sprinkles of indigenous and African religious customs mixed in. Religion typically plays a very important role in the culture. You will often hear God mentioned in daily conversation. When saying, **'Hasta luego'** (See you later) you will hear the other say, **'Si Dios quiere,'** (God-willing). The idea is that we don't have control but rather God is the commanding, omniscient character in our lives.

Yeah! Another religious Holiday!

Another way that the religion affects the culture is the impressive quantity of holidays. If you happen to work in one of these countries you will enjoy many days off and when you ask the natives the reason for the holiday, many times they are not really sure, probably celebrating a saint, they will say. Celebrations and holidays do play a large role in Spanish-speaking cultures. From the running of the bulls in Spain to the celebration of *Carnaval* throughout Latin America. There are many culturally colorful celebrations and holidays to be enjoyed.

Gesticular Differentiation

Another important aspect to mention is the different types of gestures, facial expressions, and body languages used in these cultures. In general, I have found that people are more animated and use their hands much more to gesture when talking. It is common to see two people in the street that appear to be having a heated argument and then you later find out they were just discussing the recent change in the weather. Something interesting I have noticed as well is that in some countries the people will point with their lips instead of their fingers. When greeting, many people also will kiss once on the cheek (twice in Spain starting with the left one). Men with other men typically will shake hands or hug if they are close. You will find people are generally much more affectionate, touchier, and may not respect the personal space that we are so used to having.

Learning to live in lack of luxury

Lastly, something I have found travelling to almost any other country is that we as Americans are incredibly spoiled. In no other country will you likely find the comforts and luxuries that we have in our country. And they truly are luxuries. You may find that you have to take cold showers, don't have constant access to the internet, the hotel bed is hard as a rock, or in general the area is not as clean as you are used to. You will have to remember to have an open mind, don't whine, and be incredibly thankful for what you do have.

Chapter 1
Basic Pronunciation Guidelines

I have provided two charts to help explain the pronunciation in Spanish, one containing the vowel sounds and the other the consonants. As far as vowel pronunciation goes, Spanish is much simpler than English. Spanish has five vowels that do not change. So you can always depend on the 'a' sounding like 'ah' and the 'i' sounding like 'ee', etc. English, on the other hand, also has five vowels but these five vowels can make up to 27 different sounds. Be thankful if you do not have to learn English as a second language. I sure am! Use these charts to help you pronounce the words throughout the books. Remember that you can also use the language websites at the end of the book or google translate. Just type the word in Spanish and click on the speaker icon to hear the pronunciation.

Vowel Pronunciation Chart

Vowel	How to say the letter	How to pronounce it in a word	As in…
a	Ah	Ah	Top
e	A	A	Bake
i	Ee	Ee	Meat
o	Oh	Oh	Boat
u	Oo	Oo	Cook

Consonant Pronunciation Chart

Consonant	How to say the letter	How to pronounce it in a word	As in…
b	bay	similar to English b	
c	say	k after *a, o,* or *u*	coke
		s after *e* or *i*	sit
ch	chay	ch	Check
d	day	a soft d (place your tongue at the back of your upper teeth)	
f	effay	f	
g	hay	h before i or e	hat

		g before a, o, u	<u>g</u>et
h	achay	silent	
j	hota	<u>h</u>	<u>H</u>im
k	kah	<u>k</u>	<u>K</u>arate
l	ellay	like English l with tongue raised to roof of mouth	
ll	doblay ellay	y	<u>Y</u>ellow
m	emmay	m	
n	ennay	n	
ñ	enyay	ny	Can<u>y</u>on
p	pay	like English p but you don't aspirate	
q	koo	k (q is always followed by u but the u is silent) Ex: quemar = kaymar	
r	eray	* at the beginning of a word you must roll your r's by vibrating tongue at roof of mouth * in the middle of a word it sounds like a soft d	
rr	erray	roll your r's as mentioned above	
s	essay	Like English s	
t	tay	a soft English t, the tongue touches the back of the upper teeth	
v	vay	like Spanish b	
q	koo	k (q is always followed by u but the u is silent) Ex: quemar = kaymar	
r	eray	* at the beginning	

		of a word you must roll your r's by vibrating tongue at roof of mouth * in the middle of a word it sounds like a soft d	
rr	erray	roll your r's as mentioned above	
s	essay	Like English s	
t	tay	a soft English t, the tongue touches the back of the upper teeth	
v	vay	like Spanish b	
w	doblevay	like English w	
x	equis	*Between vowels and at the end of a word, it sounds like the English *ks*. *At the beginning of a word, it sounds like the letter *s*.	*fo<u>x</u> *<u>s</u>at
y	igriega	like English y	<u>Y</u>ellow
z	sayta	s	<u>S</u>at

Grammar

When discussing the grammar of any foreign language you are learning, it is always important to understand that languages do not translate word for word. They translate as whole ideas instead. You will find some of the differences in the language structure of English and Spanish in this section. It always helps when learning a new language to be able to compare it to your own. In this grammar section I have divided it into eight parts of speech: nouns, pronouns, verbs, adjectives, adverbs, prepositions, conjunctions, and articles. I have also included in this grammar section the categories of word order, diminutives, capitalization and a list of conjugations of commonly used verbs.

-Parts of Speech
- Word Order
- Diminutives
- Capitalization
- Verb Conjugation List

Parts of Speech

Nouns

In Spanish the nouns are either feminine or masculine. It has nothing to do with the word's meaning. For example the word *make-up* (**el maquillaje**) is masculine and the word *beard* **(la barba**) is feminine.

Ex: Masculine noun

el libro = the book

Feminine noun

la cosa = the thing

Pronouns

Less Frequent use of Pronouns (I, he, she, we, it, they, etc.): Because of the verb changes mentioned below, you do not have to use pronouns as often. Instead of saying *tú corres*, (you run) you can just say *corres* because we already know that is you who we are talking about from the verb conjugation. In this book, I include both kinds of sentences, with and without the pronouns.

Formal You: There is a formal way to say *you* (Usted usually written Ud.) that is used to show respect to your elders or those in a higher position than you or simply for those whom you don't know well. I used both the informal you (tú) and the formal you (Ud.) throughout this book.

Personal Pronouns

I	Yo

You	Tú
he, she, you (formal)	Él, Ella, Usted (Ud.)
We	Nosotros (masculine) Nosotras (feminine)
You all (informal)	Vosotros (masculine) Vosotras (feminine)
They, you all	Ellos (masculine), Ellas (feminine), Ustedes (Uds.)

¡**Ojo!** Nosotras is used when it is a group of only females, Nosotros is for only males or a group of mixed gender. The same goes for Ellas/Ellas and Vosotros/Vosotras.

Verbs

Spanish has more verb changes. The verb 'hablar' (to talk) changes 6 times in the present tense. I talk (hablo) you talk (hablas) he or she talks (habla) you all talk (habláis) we talk (hablamos) they or you all talk (hablan). These are called conjugations. For this reason, Spanish also uses personal pronouns much less as I just mentioned. Later in this chapter, I will provide a list of the verb conjugations of the most used verbs in Spanish.

Adjectives

Adjectives describe a noun. The adjectives in Spanish must agree with the gender (feminine or masculine) and the number (singular or plural).

Ex:

El cuadern**o** blanc**o** = The white notebook

Las sill**as** amarill**as** = The yellow chairs

Adverbs

Adverbs describe an adjective or a verb. Most of the time, to make an adjective an adverb in Spanish, you take the feminine, singular form and add 'mente' to the end of it. Most adverbs end in 'mente' in Spanish just like most end in 'ly' in English. If an adjective stays the same in the feminine and masculine form, then you just add 'mente.' Such as 'recently.' The adjective is 'reciente' in both masculine and feminine forms, so it changes to 'recientemente' to become an adverb. Of course not all adverbs will end in 'mente' just like not all adverbs in English end in 'ly'.

Ex:

Lento (Slow) to Lentamente (Slowly)
Rápido (Fast) to Rápidamente (Quickly)
Real (Real) to Realmente (Really)

List of Irregular Adverbs

Quite	Bastante
Too/too much	Demasiado
Badly	Mal
A lot	Mucho
Very	Muy
Never	Nunca
Worse	Peor
Little	Poco
Always	Siempre

Prepositions

As I remember learning in elementary school, prepositions are what a squirrel can go... a tree (around, in, over, to, under, etc.) Of course, there are some prepositions that don't fit into that category but it was a good start as an eight year old. In most cases, prepositions in Spanish are used in sentences in a similar way as they are in English. However, most prepositions do not translate easily from English to Spanish or vice versa. Below I have a list of common prepositions.

Common Prepositions

to, at, by means of	A
Before	Antes de
Under	Bajo
Near	Cerca de
With	Con

Against	Contra
Of	De
In front of	Delante de
Inside	Dentro de
Since, from	Desde
After	Después de
Behind	Detrás de
During	Durante
In, on	En
On top of	Encima de
In front of	Enfrente de
Between, among	Entre
Outside of	Fuera de
Toward	Hacia
Until	Hasta
For, in order to	Para
For, by	Por
According to	Según
Without	Sin
Over, about	Sobre
After, behind	Tras

Conjunctions

Conjunctions provide links between words and/or groups of words. What was the conjunction in that previous sentence? You are right! It is 'and/or.' Conjunctions are used in a similar way in both Spanish and English.

So, then	Entonces
Or	O
Either...or	O...o
Neither...nor	No...ni...ni
But	Pero
And	Y

Articles

The Articles in English include 'the', 'a', and 'an.' In Spanish, on the other hand, there are eight different articles. Four of them mean 'the' and four mean 'a' or 'an.' They are said differently according to gender (masculine or feminine) and number (singular or plural). The articles are below and categorized accordingly.

Definite Articles in Spanish (The)

The	Masculine	Feminine
Singular	El	La
Plural	Los	Las

¡Ojo! 'El,' 'la,' 'los,' and 'las' all mean 'the' in English.

Ex:

el libro --- the booK
la cosa --- the thing
los libros --- the book
las cosas --- the things

The articles are much more common in Spanish. Many times when you wouldn't say   them in English, you need to say them in Spanish.

Ex:

Chocolate is my favorite. = El chocolate es mi favorito.

In English we don't say, 'The chocolate is my favorite...' but in Spanish, you do.

Indefinite Articles in Spanish (A/an)

The	Masculine	Feminine
Singular	Un	Una
Plural	Unos	Unas

¡Ojo! 'Un,' and 'Una,' both mean 'a' in English. And 'Unos,' and 'Unas' both mean 'some.'

Ex:

un libro --- a book

una cosa --- a thing

unos libros --- some books

unas cosas --- some things

The word order in Spanish is often different than it is in English. In general, it is also more flexible in Spanish than in English. For example, descriptive adjectives (ones that describe a quality of something) usually go after the noun. Instead of the *black dog*, it is the *dog black* (**perro negro**). Adjectives that describe the quantity usually go in front of the nouns (**Muchos libros, Tres personas**). Along with this, direct and indirect object pronouns can go before or after the verb. In English, the word order is typically quite strict: Subject followed by a verb and verb followed by an object if the verb has an object (I like him.) In Spanish, the subject can be omitted if it is understood (We already mentioned how subject pronouns can be omitted.) The subject can also go at the end of the sentence. For example: **'La casa la construyó Pedro.'** (Pedro built the house.) Notice how the subject 'Pedro' is at the end of the sentence. The subject could either go at the beginning or at the end.

Ex:

Adjective Noun Word Order

Tengo muchos amigos buenos. (I have many good friends.)

Notice the adjective describing quantity 'muchos' goes before the noun and the descriptive adjective 'buenos' goes after.

Direct/Indirect Object Pronouns

Me lo regaló mi amiga. (My friend gave it to me.)

The sentence literally says, 'Me it gave my friend.'

The subject goes at the end of the sentence as well.

Omission of Subject

Mi papá es muy alto. Tiene 55 años. (My dad is very tall. He is 55.)

In the second sentence, 'he' is left out since we already know who the sentence is about.

Subject at the end of the sentence

El carro lo arregló el mecánico. (The mechanic fixed the car.)

The subject 'the mechanic' is found at the end of the sentence and the object 'the car' is at the beginning.

Diminutives (Word endings)

Diminutives are very commonly added to words especially the diminutive 'ito' which is used to say something in a cuter way or to talk about something that is a small. For example, the cute little dog (el perrito) but it is used much more frequently than in English and can be added to adjectives and nouns. It is often used to show affection, **'Mi amorcito'** (My little love).

Capitalization

Many words that are capitalized in English are not in Spanish. For example, days of the week, months, languages and nationalities.

Ex: English = inglés
Colombian =   colombiano
Thursday = el jueves
March = marzo

Verb Conjugation List

Below you will find conjugations of some of the most commonly used verbs in Spanish. You can use it as a reference as you read through the book or on your travels.

Ir- to go

Yo --**Voy** -- **I go**
Tú -- **Vas** -- **you go**

él, ella, Ud. -- **Va** -- **She, she goes; you (formal) go; it goes**

nosotros, nosotras -- **Vamos** -- **we go**

vosotras, vosotras -- **Vais - you (plural) go**

ellos, ellas, Uds. -- **Van** -- **they, you all go**

Tener- to have

Yo -- **Tengo** -- **I have**

Tú -- **Tienes** -- **you have**

él, ella, Ud -- **Tiene** -- **he, she has; you (formal) have; it has**

nosotros, nosotras -- **Tenemos** -- **we have**

vosotras, vosotras -- **Tenéis** -- **you (plural) have**

ellos, ellas, Uds -- **Tienen** -- **they, you all have, '**

*In order to say 'to have to' just say 'tener que'

Ex: Tengo que ir = I have to go.

Salir- To leave/go out

Yo -- **Salgo** -- **I leave**

tú -- **Sales** -- **you leave**

él, ella, Ud. -- **Sale** -- **he, she leaves; you (formal) leave; it leaves**

nosotros, nosotras -- **Salimos** -- **we leave**

vosotras, vosotras -- **Salís** -- **you (plural) leave**

ellos, ellas, Uds. -- **Salen** -- **they, you all leave**

Ser- to be (permanent)

Yo -- **Soy** -- **I am**

tú -- **Eres** -- **you are**

él, ella, Ud. -- **Es** -- **he, she is; you (formal) are; it is**

nosotros, nosotras -- **Somos** -- **we are**

vosotras, vosotras -- **Sois** -- **you (plural) are**

ellos, ellas, Uds. -- **Son** -- **they, you all are**

Estar- to be (Temporary)

Yo -- **Estoy** -- **I am**

tú -- **Estás** -- **you are**

él, ella, Ud. -- **Está -- he, she is; you (formal) are; it is**

nosotros, nosotras -- **Estamos -- we are**

vosotras, vosotras -- **Estáis -- you (plural) are**

ellos, ellas, Uds. -- **Están -- they, you all are**

Poder- to be able to

Yo -- **Puedo -- I can**

tú -- **Puedes -- you can**

él, ella, Ud. -- **Puede -- he, she can; you (formal) can**

nosotros, nosotras -- **Podemos -- we can**

vosotras, vosotras -- **Podéis -- you (plural) can**

ellos, ellas, Uds. -- **Pueden -- they, you all can**

*In order to say: I can do something, just add the *infinitive* after the form of *poder*.

Ex:

I can go today = Puedo ir hoy

We can see my mom. = Podemos ver a mi mama.

Querer- to want

Yo -- **Quiero -- I want**

tú -- **Quieres -- you want**

él, ella, Ud. -- **Quiere -- he, she wants; you (formal) want**

nosotros, nosotras -- **Queremos -- we want**

vosotras, vosotras -- **Queréis -- you (plural) want**

ellos, ellas, Uds. -- **Quieren -- they, you all want**

Saber- to know

Yo -- **Sé -- I know**

tú -- **Sabes -- you know**

él, ella, Ud. -- **Sabe -- he, she knows; you (formal) know**

nosotros, nosotras -- **Sabemos -- we know**

vosotras, vosotras -- **Sabéis -- you (plural) know**

ellos, ellas, Uds. -- **Saben -- they, you all know**

Hacer- to do/to make

Yo -- **Hago -- I do/make**
Tú -- **Haces -- you do/make**
él, ella, Ud. -- **Hace -- he, she does/makes; you (formal) do/make**
nosotros, nosotras -- **Hacemos -- we do/make**
vosotras, vosotras -- **Hacéis -- you (plural) do/make**
ellos, ellas, Uds -- **Hacen -- they, you do/make**

Deber- must/should

Yo -- **Debo -- I should**
tú -- **Debes -- you should**
él, ella, Ud. -- **Debe -- he, she ,you (formal) should**
nosotros, nosotras -- **Debemos -- we should**
vosotras, vosotras -- **Debéis -- you (plural) should**
ellos, ellas, Uds. -- **Deben -- they, you all should**

Hablar – to talk

Yo -- **Hablo -- I talk**
tú -- **Hablas -- you talk**
él, ella, Ud. -- **Habla -- he, she talks; you (formal) talk**
nosotros, nosotras -- **Hablamos -- we talk**
vosotras, vosotras -- **Habláis -- you (plural) talk**
ellos, ellas, Uds. -- **Hablan -- they, you all talk**

Necesitar- to need

Yo -- **Necesito -- I need**
tú -- **Necesitas -- you need**
él, ella, Ud. -- **Necesita -- he, she needs; you (formal) need**
nosotros, nosotras -- **Necesitamos - we need**
vosotras, vosotras -- **Necesitáis -- you (plural) need**
ellos, ellas, Uds. -- **Necesitan -- they, you need**

Pensar- to think

Yo -- **Pienso -- I think**

Tú -- **Piensas -- you think**

él, ella, Ud. -- **Piensa -- he, she thinks; you (formal) think**

nosotros, nosotras -- **Pensamos -- we think**

vosotras, vosotras -- **Penséis -- you (plural) think**

ellos, ellas, Uds. -- **Piensan -- they, you all think**

Decir- to say

Yo -- **Digo -- I say**

Tú -- **Dices -- you say**

él, ella, Ud. -- **Dice -- he, she says; you (formal) say**

vosotras, vosotras -- **Decís -- you (plural) say**

nosotros, nosotras -- **Decimos -- we say**

ellos, ellas, Uds. -- **Dicen -- they, you say**

* I included a conjugation of *decir* in the past tense due to its frequence of use.

Decir- to say (Past tense)

Yo -- **Dije --I said/told**

tú -- **Dijiste -- you said/told**

él, ella, Ud.-- **Dijo -- he, she said/told; you (formal) said/told**

vosotras, vosotras -- **Dijisteis -- you (plural) said/told**

nosotros, nosotras -- **Dijimos -- we said/told**

ellos, ellas, Uds. -- **Dijeron -- they, you said/told**

Useful phrases using Decir

(él/ella) me dijo	(he/she) told me
te dije	I told you
le dije	I told (him/her/you)
Les dije	I told (them/you all)

Gustar- to like

The verb 'gustar- to like' is conjugated in a different way. The reason for this is that when you say, 'I like' in Spanish, you are actually saying 'it is pleasing to me.' Below, I will outline the ways to use gustar with different people.

A mí -- **me gusta**... -- I like...

A ti -- **te gusta**... -- You like...

A él -- **le gusta**... -- He likes...

A ella -- **le gusta**... -- She likes...

A nosotros/as -- **nos gusta**... -- We like...

A vosotros/as -- **os gusta**... -- You (plural) like...

A ellos/as -- **les gusta**... -- They like...

A Uds. -- **les gusta...** -- You all like...

¡Ojo!   It is not necessary to say the first two words (*A mí, a tí, etc.*) you can just say *me gusta, te gusta, etc.*

Ex:

I like to read. =Me gusta leer

¡Bonus!

Useful verbs/words I use throughout this book

¿Quisieras...? = Would you like...?
Quisiera... = I would like...
¿Te gustaría...? = Would you like..?
Me gustaría... = I would like...
¿Quieres...? = Do you want...?
Quiero... = I want...
Necesito... = I need...
Busco... = I am looking for...
¡Ojo! = Be careful! Watch out/Pay attention to this!

Most Useful Words and Phrases

Below, I will list some general useful phrases and words. These phrases and words will be divided into several categories to make them easier to locate. These categories are listed below.

-Question Words
-Most Commonly Used Words
-Phrases to use when confused
-Friendly phrases

-Exclamations

-Time expressions

-More random useful phrases

-Colors and numbers

Question Words

What?	¿Qué?
Where?	¿Dónde?
When?	¿Cuándo?
Which?	¿Cuál?
Why?	¿Por qué?
Who?	¿Quién?

¡Ojo! When questions words are used in a question, they have an accent.

Ex: ¿Quién es? = Who is it?

When question words are used in a statement they don't carry an accent.

Ex:

Es mi amiga quien es una profesora. = It is my friend who is a teacher.

Most Commonly Used Words

Yes	Sí

No	No
But	Pero
Also/Too	También
Is	Es (permanent)
	Está (temporary)
Now	Ahora
Because	Porque
Well	Pues/Bueno
So/then	Entonces
Sorry	Lo siento
Excuse me	Perdón
Thank you	Gracias
You're welcome	De nada
Please	Por favor
Me too.	Yo también
Very	Muy
A lot	Mucho
That's okay/That's fine/Okay	Está bien
That's okay/okay	Vale
Like this/that	Así

Phrases to use when confused

I don't understand.	No entiendo.
Can you repeat, please?	¿Puede repetir, por favor?
Speak more slowly, please.	Hable más despacio, por favor.
How do you say…?	¿Cómo se dice…?
What does this mean?	¿Qué significa esto?
What is this?	¿Qué es esto?
Can you help me?	¿Me puede ayudar?
Do you speak English?	¿Habla inglés?
I speak a little Spanish.	Hablo un poco de español.
I don't know.	No sé.
Write it down, please.	Escríbalo por favor.
I have no idea.	No tengo ni idea.
I need to practice my Spanish.	Me falta práctica en español.

Friendly phrases

Hey, friend!	¡Eh, Amigo!
Welcome	Bienvenido(s)
Long time no see!	¡Tanto tempo!
Good luck!	¡Buena suerte!
Have a nice day!	¡Que pase un buen día!
I love you.	Te quiero/Te amo
I missed you so much!	¡Te extrañe mucho!
You are very kind!	¡Eres muy amable!
What's new?	¿Qué hay de nuevo?
Not much.	Nada.
Wait for me!	¡Espéreme!
Come with me!	¡Ven conmigo!
Follow me!	¡Sígueme!
Call me.	Llámame.
Get well soon!	Que te mejores pronto.
Merry Christmas!	¡Feliz Navidad!
Happy New Year!	¡Feliz Año Nuevo!
Happy Birthday!	¡Feliz cumpleaños!
Happy Easter!	¡Feliz Pascua!

Exclamations

Goodness!	¡Caramba!
Oh my god!	¡Ay Dios mío!
Congratulations!	¡Felicidades!
That's good!	¡Que bien! or ¡Que Bueno!
How wonderful!	¡Que maravilloso!
How beautiful!	¡Que hermoso!
How pretty!	¡Que bonito!
That's no good!	¡Que malo!
That's horrible!	¡Que horrible!
What a shame!	¡Que lástima!
What a mess!	¡Que lío!
Leave me alone!	¡Déjenme en paz!
Careful!	¡Ojo!

Time Expressions

Before	Antes

Now	Ahora
After	Después
Later/Then	Luego

One moment, please.	Un momento, por favor.
Stay there, I am going to take a photo.	Párese allí, voy a sacarte una foto.
Say hi to Ana for me.	Dále saludos a Ana (de mi parte)
Do you like it here?	¿Le gusta aquí?
It is a wonderful country.	Es un país maravilloso.
I have been learning Spanish for 2 months.	Tengo dos meses estudiando español.
Bless you! (When sneezing)	¡Salud!
God bless you!	¡Que dios le bendiga!
Don't worry!	¡No te preocupes!
Can you hold this, please?	¿Me ayuda a cargar esto, por favor?
Where are you going?	¿Adónde vas?
I am going home.	Voy a mi casa.

Colors and Numbers

Colors

Red	Rojo/a
Orange	Anaranjado/a
Yellow	Amarillo/a
Green	Verde
Blue	Azúl
Purple	Morado/a
Pink	Rosado/a
Black	Negro/a
White	Blanco/a
Brown	Marrón
Gray	Gris

Numbers 1-10

1	uno

2	dos
3	tres
4	cuatro
5	cinco
6	seis
7	siete
8	ocho
9	nueve
10	diez

Numbers 11-20

11	once
12	doce
13	trece
14	catorce
15	quince
16	dieciseis
17	diecisiete
18	dieciocho
19	diecinueve
20	veinte

¡Ojo! 21-29 follows this pattern: veinti + number as one word

Ex:

21 = veintiuno

22 = veintidos

23 = veintitres, etc.

Numbers 30-100+

30	treinta
40	cuarenta
50	cincuenta
60	sesenta

70	setenta
80	ochenta
90	noventa
100	cien
105	ciento cinco
115	ciento quince

¡Ojo! 31-99 follows this pattern: treinta + number as two separate words

Ex:

39 = treinta y nueve

57 = cincuenta y siete

92 = noventa y dos,

* In order to say, 101 to 199, just say ciento + the number

Ex:
185 = ciento ochenta y cinco

Numbers 200-1000

200	doscientos
300	trescientos
400	cuatrocientos
500	**quinientos**
600	seiscientos
700	**setecientos**
800	ochocientos
900	**novecientos**
1000	mil

¡Ojo! Notice how the the numbers in bold change.

Chapter 2
Travelling, Lodging & How to Find Your Way Around

In this chapter, I provide you with language to help to get set up when you first arrive to your country. It includes sections on the airport, public transportation, finding accommodation and directions.

-In the Airport
-Public Transportation
-Finding Accommodation
-Wandering Around

In the Airport

This part will discuss that exciting moment when you arrive to the new country ready for an adventure full of potential and wonder. I will list useful vocabulary and phrases for you to use in order to get in and out of that airport and into your country or away to travel. Bon voyage or as they say in Spanish, *Buen Viaje*!

Airport Phrases

Airplane	El Avión
May I see your passport?	¿Puedo ver su pasaporte?
We just arrived to the airport	Acabamos de llegar al aeropuerto
Which airline?	¿Cuál aerolínea?
My suitcases are lost.	Mis maletas están perdidas.
Customs	La aduana
Here is your ticket	Tome su boleto
What is your final destination?	¿Cuál es su destino?
What time does the flight leave?	¿A qué hora sale el vuelo?
What time does the flight arrive?	¿A qué hora llega el vuelo?
You are late!	¡Usted está atrasado!
You should hurry!	¡Debe darse prisa!
Really?	¿De verdad?
How many suitcases do you have?	¿Cuántas maletas tiene?
I have one suitcase.	Tengo una maleta
Your suitcase is too heavy.	Su maleta está sobrepeso.

You will have to remove some things.	Tiene que sacar algunas cosas.
Where is terminal E?	¿Dónde está la terminal E?
I´m looking for gate 27.	Busco la puerta 27.
Where is the baggage claim?	¿Dónde está el reclamo de equipaje?
My suitcases are lost.	Mis maletas están perdidas.
Have a good trip!	¡Buen viaje!
Enjoy your flight!	Disfrute su vuelo

¡Los Ejercicios!

Find with the word from the word bank to fill in the blank and translate to English

la maleta -- destino -- La terminal --
sobrepeso -- La aerolínea -- aeropuerto

1. La maleta está _____

2. ¿Cuál es su _____ final? -
_____

3. Acabamos de llegar al _____. -
_____

4. ¿Dónde está _____ B?
_____

5. Tiene una _____ que está sobrepeso.

Match the Vocabulary

6. El vuelo --- a. Ticket
7. El Reclamo de Equipaje --- b. Airplane
8. El boleto --- c. Enjoy your flight.
9. El avión --- d. Baggage Claim
10. Disfrute su vuelo --- e. Flight

Translate to English

- Hola, ¿a qué hora sale su vuelo?
- Hola, Sale a las cuatro de la tarde.
- ¡Ud. está atrasado! ¡Debe darse prisa!
- ¿De verdad?
- ¿Cuántas maletas tiene?
- Tengo dos maletas.
- Una maleta está sobrepeso. Tiene que sacar algunas cosas.
- Está bien, señor. Muchas gracias.
- De nada. ¡Disfrute su vuelo!

In the Airport Answers

Fill in the blank with the word from the word bank

1. La maleta está <u>sobrepeso</u>. ------ <u>The suitcase is too heavy.</u>
2. ¿Cuál es su <u>destino</u> final? ------ <u>What is your final destination?</u>
3. Acabamos de llegar al <u>aeropuerto</u>. ------ <u>We just arrived to the airport.</u>
4. ¿Dónde está <u>la terminal</u> B? ------ <u>Where is terminal B?</u>
5. Tiene una <u>maleta</u> que está sobrepeso. ------ <u>You have a suitcase that is too heavy.</u>

Match the Vocabulary

6. El vuelo ------ e. Flight
7. El Reclamo de Equipaje ------ d. Baggage Claim
8. El boleto------ a. Ticket
9. El avión ------ b. Airplane
10. Disfrute su vuelo ------ c. Enjoy your flight

Translate to English

- Hola, ¿a qué hora sale su vuelo? ------ Hello, what time does your flight leave?
- Hola, Sale a las cuatro de la tarde. ------ Hello, It leaves at four p.m.
- ¡Ud. está atrasado! ¡Debe darse prisa! ------ You are late! You have to hurry!
- ¿De verdad? ------ Really?
- ¿Cuántas maletas tiene? ------ How many suitcases do you have?
- Tengo dos maletas. ------ I have two suitcases.
- Una maleta está sobrepeso. ------ One suitcase is overweight.
- Tiene que sacar algunas cosas. ------ You have to take some things out.
- Está bien, señor. Muchas gracias. ------ Okay, sir. Thank you so much.

- De nada. ¡Disfrute su vuelo! ------ Your welcome. Enjoy your flight!

Public Transportation

This section is dedicated to the time when you get out of the airport and need to know how to get around, so as soon as you hop in that cab, bus or train, you know how to say what you need to make it to your destination. Most people these days use the GPS on their smart phone so don't even have to think about trying to find their way around. Unfortunately, or maybe fortunately, in your Spanish-speaking country, you may not have that easy access to internet and therefore will have to talk to real people and ask for directions. Here are some useful phrases and vocabulary to help you get around the city!

Taking Taxis

Where do you want to go?	¿Adónde quiere ir?
Where are we going?	¿Adónde vamos?
I'm going to the … hotel	Voy al hotel …
Do you know where … is?	¿Sabe donde está …?
Take me to this address, please	Lléveme a esta dirección, por favor
Where are the taxis?	¿Dónde están los taxis?
Is it far?	¿Es lejos?
Is it near?	¿Es cerca?
Go that way.	Vaya por allá.
Keep going straight.	Sigue derecho
Go straight for three blocks.	Sigue derecho por tres cuadras
At the stoplight, turn right/left	En el semáforo, dobla a la derecha/a la izquierda
You can stop here.	Puede parar aqui.
Here on the right/left	Aquí a la derecha/izquierda
How much do I owe you?	¿Cuánto le debo?

Buses, Trains, and Subways oh my!

Where is the subway?	¿Dónde está el metro?
Where is the bus?	¿Por dónde pasa el autobús?
A map of the city, please.	Un mapa de la ciudad, por favor.
The bus/train station	La estación de bus/tren
When does the next train leave for…?	¿A qué hora sale el próximo tren

	para...?
Bus stop	La parada de bus
Departures	Salidas
Arrivals	Llegadas
I would like a one way ticket	Quisiera un boleto de ida.
Round trip ticket	Boleto de ida y vuelta
Platform	Andén
Which platform does the train leave from?	¿De cuál andén sale el tren?
Do I need to change trains?	¿Necesito cambiar de tren?
To get on/in...	Subir
To get off.	Bajar

¡Los Ejercicios!

Fill in the blank with the correct vocabulary word and translate to English.

1. Necesito _____ de tren. ------ (ir, cambiar, llegar, parar)
2. ¿A qué hora _____ el próximo tren para Madrid? ------ (sale, ida, ir, sigue)
3. ¿De cuál _____ sale el tren? ------ (salida, llegada, andén, ida)
4. Quisiera un boleto de _____. ------ (ciudad, dirección, ida, salida)
5. Lléveme a esta _____, por favor. ------ (tren, andén, dirección, boleto)

Match the Phrases

6. Voy a este hotel. ------ a. Keep going straight.
7. Boleto de ida y vuelta------ b. I am going to this hotel.
8. Sigue derecho. ------ c. To get on the train
9. Subir al tren. ------ d.Round tripticket
10. En el semáforo dobla a la izquierda. ------ e. At the stoplight, turn left.

*Review the conjugation of the verb Salir in the Grammar Section.

*Remember in order to say the third person singular, *it leaves,* you use the third conjugation, *sale.*

Ex:

El autobús **sale** en dos horas. = The bus **leaves** in 2 hours.

El tren **sale** a las 9:00.　　　　=　　　　The train **leaves** at 9:00.

Conjugate the verb *salir*.

11. ¿A qué hora _____ el bus para Toledo?
12. El bus _____ a las diez de la mañana?
13. ¿Tú _____ hoy para la casa de tu abuela?
14 Yo _____ para Barcelona en tres horas.
15. ¿Cuándo _____ ellos para Córdoba?

Find the correct sentence for each group and translate.

1.
___¿Cuándo están los taxis?
___¿Dónde están los taxis?
___¿Qué están lost taxis?

_____

2.
___ Quisiera un boleto de andén.
___ Quisiera un boleto de llegada
___ Quisiera un boleto de ida y vuelta.

_____

3.
___ ¿Sabe donde está la parada de bus?
___ ¿Sabe la parada de bus donde está ...?
___ ¿Sabe cuando está la parada de bus?

_____

4.
___ ¿A qué hora salgo el autobús?
___ ¿A qué hora sale el autobús?
___ ¿A qué hora salimos el autobús?

_____

Public Transportation **Answers**

Fill in the blank with the correct vocabulary word and translate to English.

1. Necesito <u>cambiar</u> de tren. ------ (ir, <u>cambiar</u>, llegar, parar)
2. ¿A qué hora <u>sale</u> el próximo tren para Madrid? ------ (<u>sale,</u> ida, ir, sigue)
3. ¿De cuál <u>andén</u> sale el tren? ------ (salida, llegada, <u>andén</u>, ida)
4. Quisiera un boleto de <u>ida</u>. ------ (ciudad, dirección, <u>ida</u>, salida)
5. Lléveme a esta <u>dirección</u>, por favor. ------ (tren, andén, <u>dirección</u>, boleto)

Match the Phrases

6. Voy a este hotel. ------ b. I am going to this hotel.
7. Boleto de ida y vuelta------ d.Round tripticket
8. Sigue derecho. ------ a. Keep going straight.
9. Subir al tren. ------ c. To get on the train
10. En el semáforo dobla a la izquierda. ------ e. At the stoplight, turn left.

Conjugate the verb *salir*.

11. ¿A qué hora <u>sale</u> el bus para Toledo?
12. El bus <u>sale</u> a las diez de la mañana?
13. ¿Tú <u>sales</u> hoy para la casa de tu abuela?
14 Yo <u>salgo</u> para Barcelona en tres horas.
15. ¿Cuándo <u>salen</u> ellos para Córdoba?

Find the correct sentence for each group and translate.

1.
___¿Cuándo están los taxis?
x¿Dónde están los taxis?
___¿Qué están lost taxis?   <u>Where are the taxis?-</u>
_____

2.
___ Quisiera un boleto de andén.
___ Quisiera un boleto de llegada
x Quisiera un boleto de ida y vuelta.   <u>I would like a roundtrip</u>
<u>ticket._____</u>
3.
<u>x</u> ¿Sabe donde está la parada de bus?
___ ¿Sabe la parada de bus donde está ...?

___ ¿Sabe cuando está la parada de bus?   Do you know where the bus stop
is?
4.
___ ¿A qué hora salgo el autobús?
x ¿A qué hora sale el autobús?
___ ¿A qué hora salimos el autobús?   What time does the bus
leave?

Finding Accommodation

Once you have made your way to where you are going, you now need to book
room and board. These phrases will help you in your hotel, hostel, bed and
breakfast, or wherever you have decided to stay. Remember the
accommodation in foreign countries may not be as luxurious or convenient as
you are used to. Here some phrases to help you enjoy your stay!

Hotel Vocabulary

I would like to reserve a room for one/two people.	Quisiera reservar una habitación para una/dos personas
How much does it cost per night?	¿Cuánto cuesta por noche?
For how many people?	¿Para cuántas personas?
For how many nights?	¿Para cuántas noches?
Para una noche/dos noches	For one night/two nights
With a double bed.	Con una cama de matrimonio.
With two single beds	Con dos camas sencillas
I'm sorry, we are full.	Lo siento, está todo vendido
I have a reservation.	Tengo una reserva.
Enjoy your stay!	¡Disfrute su estadía!

Hotel Meals

Is breakfast included?	¿Está incluido el desayuno?
When is breakfast?	¿A qué hora es el desayuno?
Lunch	El almuerzo
Dinner	La cena

Hotel Ammenities

Do you have wi-fi?	¿Tiene wi-fi?
Is there a gym?	¿Hay gimnasio?
Is there a laundromat nearby?	¿Hay una lavandería cerca?
Is there a safe deposit box?	¿Hay una caja fuerte?
Is there air-conditioning?	¿Hay aire acondicionado?
Is there a shuttle to the airport?	¿Hay transporte del hotel al aeropuerto?
Can you wake me up at 6?	¿Me puede despertar a las seis?

The Word 'hay' sounds like the letter I.

¿Qué necesitas? (What do you need?)

I need...	Necesito...
clean towels	toallas limpias
toilet paper	papel de baño
soap	jabón
a blanket	una manta
hangers	perchas

¡Los Ejercicios!

Find out if sentences are *correcto* or *incorrecto,* correct, and then translate.

1. Quisiera reservo una habitación para tres personas.

_____

2. ¿Puede una caja fuerte?

_____

3. ¿Hay transporte del hotel al aeropuerto?

_____

4. Necesito papel de baño.

_____

5. ¿Me puede despertar las seis?

_____

Match the Phrases to their English translation

6. Necesito toallas limpias. ------ a. Is breakfast included?
7. ¿Está incluido el desayuno? ------ b. Is there a safe?
8. ¿Hay una caja fuerte? ------ c. How much is it a night?
9. Necesito unas perchas ------ d. I need clean towels.
10. ¿Cuánto cuesta por noche? ------ e. I need some hangers.

Translate to English
- Buenas tardes señor. ¿Cómo le puedo ayudar?
- Buenas tardes, señora.
- Quisiera reservar una habitación para dos personas.
- ¿Cuántas noches, necesita Ud.?
- Necesito una noche. Y con dos camas sencillas.
- Vale.
- ¿Hay aire acondicionado?
- Sí, también hay un gimnasio.
- ¡Que bueno! ¿Me puede despertar a las cinco?
- Por supuesto, señor.
- Muchas gracias.
- De nada

Finding Accommodation Answers

Find out if sentences are *correcto* or *incorrecto*, correct, and then translate.

1. Quisiera reserv**ar** una habitación para tres personas

Correcto - I would like to reserve a room for for three people.

2. ¿**Hay** una caja fuerte?

Correcto - Is there a safe?

3. ¿Hay transporte del hotel al aeropuerto?

Correcto- Is there transportation from the hotel to the airport?

4. Necesito papel de baño.

Correcto- I need toilet paper.

5. ¿Me puede despertar **a** las seis?

Incorrecto - Can you wake me up at six?

Match the Phrases to their English translation

6. Necesito toallas limpias. ------ d. I need clean towels.
7. ¿Está incluido el desayuno? ------ a. Is breakfast included?
8. ¿Hay una caja fuerte? ------ b. Is there a safe?
9. Necesito unas perchas ------ e. I need some hangers.
10. ¿Cuánto cuesta por noche? ------   c. How much is it a night?

Translate to English

- Buenas tardes señor. ¿Cómo le puedo ayudar?
- Good afternoon, sir. How can I help you?
- Buenas tardes, señora.
- Good afternoon, ma'am.
- Quisiera reservar una habitación para dos personas.
- I would like to reserve a room for 2 people.
- ¿Cuántas noches, necesita Ud.? Necesito una noche.Y con dos camas sencillas.
- How many nights do you need?
- I need one night. And two single beds.
- Vale.
- Okay.
- ¿Hay aire acondicionado?
- Is there air conditioning?
- Sí, también hay un gimnasio. ¡Que bueno! ¿Me puede despertar a las cinco?
- Yes, there is also a gym.
- Good! Can you wake me up at five?
- Por supuesto, señor.
- Of course, sir.
- Muchas gracias.
- Thank you so much.
- De nada
- You're welcome.

Wandering Around

These phrases will help you ask for directions and learn how to say several places found in the city. Don't forget to say, *'Más despacio, por favor,"* if the directions you are given sound faster than light travel. Most natives will be kind and patient enough to make sure you understand. So here are your direction phrases and make sure you don't get lost!

¿Dónde está? (Where is it?)

Excuse me, where is the…	¿Perdón dónde está el/la …?
It's next to the…	Está al lado de la/del …
It's in front of the…	Está al frente de la/ del …
Walk straight	Camina derecho
Turn right	Dobla a la derecha
Turn left	Dobla a la izquierda
It's on the right/left	Está a la derecha/ a la izquierda
Far from	Lejos de
Near to	Cerca de
Above	Encima de
Below	Debajo de
Behind	Atrás de
Where am I on the map?	¿Dónde estoy en el mapa?
On which street?	¿En qué calle está?

Lugares (Places)

Where is…?	¿Dónde está…?
The bank	El banco
The restaurant	El restaurant
The post office	El correo
The supermarket	El supermercado
The market	El mercado
The pharmacy	La farmacia
The bakery	La panadería
Bus/Train station	La estación del bus/tren
Store	La tienda
Church	La iglesia
Stationary Store	La papelería
The police station	La estación de policía
Downtown	El centro
The park	El parque
The zoo	El zoológico
The swimming pool	La piscina
The school	La escuela
The university	La universidad

The hospital	El hospital

¡Ojo! Pay attention to which words are masculine and feminine?

See the difference:

It is next to the park = Está al lado **del** parque

It is next to the school = Está al lado **de la** escuela.

Otras frases (Other phrases)

I am lost.	Estoy perdido/perdida
How do I get to …?	¿Cómo llego a…?
Cross the street.	Cruza la calle.
Where am I now?	¿Dónde estoy ahora?
the corner	la esquina
one block	una cuadra
Street	calle
here	aquí
There	ahí/allí
There	allá (farther away)

¡Los Ejercicios!

Find the correct sentence for each group and translate.

1.
____ El correo está al lado de el hospital
____ El correo está al lado de la hospital
____ El correo está al lado del hospital.

_____

2.
____ La iglesia está lejos de la papelería.
____ La iglesia está lejos del la papelería.
____ La iglesia está lejos de el papelería.

_____

3.

___ ¿Cómo llego al supermercado?
___ ¿Dónde llego al supermercado?
___ ¿Qué llego al supermercado?

_____

4.
___ El banco está al derecho.
___ La banco está al derecho.
___ El banco está a la derecha.

_____

Match the Phrases

1. I am lost. ------ a. ¿Es lejos
2. Cross the street. ------ b. Camina derecho.
3. Wa straight ------ c. ¿Dónde está el centro?
4. Where am I now? ------ d. Estoy perdida.
5. It is above the bank. ------ e. Cruza la calle.
6. Is it far? ------ f. ¿Dónde estoy ahora?
7. On which street? ------ g. Está encima del banco.
8. It is behind the pool. ------ h. ¿Está debajo del restaurante?
9. Is it underneath the.restaurant? ------ i. ¿En qué calle está?
        10. Where is downtown? ------ j. Está atrás de la piscina.

Wandering Around Answers

Find the correct sentence for each group and translate.

1.
___ El correo está al lado de el hospital
___ El correo está al lado de la hospital
x   El correo está al lado del hospital.   The post office is next to the
hospital.

2.
x La iglesia está lejos de la papelería.
___ La iglesia está lejos del la papelería.
___ La iglesia está lejos de el papelería.   The church is far from the
stationary store.

3.

x ¿Cómo llego al supermercado?

___ ¿Dónde llego al supermercado?

___ ¿Qué llego al supermercado?   How do I get to the supermarket?

4.

___ El banco está al derecho.

___ La banco está al derecho.

x El banco está a la derecha.   The bank is to the right.

Match the Phrases

1. I am lost. ------ d. Estoy perdida.

2. Cross the street. ------ e. Cruza la calle.

3. Keep straight ------ b. Sigue derecho.

4. Where am I now? ------ f. ¿Dónde estoy ahora?

5. It is above the bank. ------ g. Está encima del banco.

6. Is it far? ------ a. ¿Es lejos?

7. On which street? ------ i. ¿En qué calle está?

8. It is behind the pool. ------ j. Está atrás de la piscina.

9. Is it underneath the.restaurant? ------ h. ¿Está debajo del restaurante?

10. Where is downtown? ------ c. ¿Dónde está el centro?

.

Chapter 3
Crash Guide to Social Skills In Spanish

In this section, we will discuss how to greet, get to know each other, make friends, etc. remember that greeting in most Spanish-speaking countries includes one kiss on the cheek between females (two in Spain) and hand-shakes between men. The kiss on the cheek usually is just a light touch of the cheek and you kiss the air. Sometimes you will find that a man and woman will greet with a kiss and sometimes with just a handshake. It is usually important to make direct eye contact when greeting each other. This chapter will include phrases to help you to greet others and describe yourself, job, interests, and family. Here are some phrases to help you meet some people and make some friends!

-Meet and greet

-Describing your world

-Phrases using 'Tener"

-Occupations

-Interests

-Family Matters

Meet and greet

This section helps you to greet people, introduce yourself, and find out more about others such as their age, origin, and where they live.

Saludando (Saying Hi)

Hello	Hola
Good Morning	Buenos Días
Good Afternoon	Buenas Tardes
Good evening/Good night	Buenas Noches
General Greeting	Buenas
Have sweet dreams!	¡Dulces Sueños!

¿Cómo les va? (How are you all doing?)

How are you? (informal)	¿Cómo estás?
How are you? (formal)	¿Cómo está Ud.?
How are you doing? (informal)	¿Cómo te va?
How are you doing?(formal)	¿Cómo le va?
How are you?	¿Qué tal?
Well/Very well	Bien/Muy bien
Good and you? (informal)	¿Bien y tú?
Good and you? (formal)	¿Bien y Ud?
Excellent	Excelente
Very well	Súper bien
So-so	Así así
I'm not okay	Estoy mal/No estoy bien
Horrible	Horrible
What's up? What's new?	¿Qué hay?

Parting is such sweet sorrow

English	Spanish
Goodbye	Adiós
See you later	Hasta luego
See you tomorrow	Hasta mañana
See you soon	Hasta pronto
See you	Nos vemos
I'm going.	Me voy.
Have a good day!	¡Que tenga un buen dia!
Bye	Chau

Cuénteme más de ti (Tell me more about yourself)

What is your name? (informal)	¿Cómo te llamas?
What is your name? (formal)	¿Cómo se llama?
My name is...	Me llamo...
My name is...	Mi nombre es...
I am...	Soy...
Nice to meet you!	¡Mucho gusto!
It's a pleasure.	Es un placer.
The pleasure is mine.	El placer es mío

Me too.	Yo también
Where are you from? (informal)	¿De dónde eres?
Where are you from? (formal)	¿De dónde es?
I am from the U.S.	Soy de los estados unidos.
How old are you? (informal)	¿Cuántos años tienes?
How old are you? (formal)	¿Cuántos años tiene?
I am... years old.	Tengo ... años.
Where do you live? (informal)	¿Dónde vives?
Where do you live? (informal)	¿Dónde vive?
I live close to the ocean.	Vivo cerca al mar.
I live in the country.	Vivo en el campo.
I live in the mountains.	Vivo en las montañas.
Canada	Cánada
England	Inglaterra
South Africa	África del Sur
Australia	Australia
New Zealand	Nueva Zelanda
Spain	España
Mexico	México (the x is pronounced like an h)
Argentina	Argentina (the g is pronounced like an h)
Italy	Italia
France	Francia
Japan	Japón
China	China (Pronounced cheena)
Germany	Alemania
The Netherlands	Holanda/Países Bajos

¡Los Ejercicios!

Translate the following into English

- ¡Buenas noches amigo!
- ¡Hola! ¿Qué tal?
- Súper bien, gracias, ¿y Ud.?
- ¡Maravilloso, muchas gracias!
- ¿Cómo te llamas?
- Me llamo Juan, ¿y Ud. cómo se llama?
- Me llamo Laura.

-¿De dònde eres?
- Soy de Estados Unidos. ¿y tú?
- Soy de México.
- ¿Cuántos años tienes?
- Tengo 30 años.
-¿Y dónde vives?
-Vivo cerca del mar en Puerta Vallarta. ¿Y tú?
-Vivo en las montañas.
-¡Que bueno! Es un placer.
-¡El placer es mío!

Match the Phrases

1. Vivo en Alemania.	a. I am Joseph.
2. Mucho gusto.	b. I live in the country.
3. Soy José.	c. How's it going?
4. Vivo en el campo.	d. What's your name?
5. Soy de Inglaterra.	e. Have a good day.
6. Que tenga un buen día	f. See you.
7. ¿Qué hay?	g. I am from England.
8. ¿Cómo le va?	h. What's new?
9. Nos vemos	i. Nice to meet you.
10. ¿Cómo se llama?	j. I live in Germany.

Meet and greet Answers

Translate the following into English

-¡Buenas noches amigo!
-¡Hola! ¿Qué tal?
- Súper bien, gracias, ¿y Ud.?
-¡Maravilloso, muchas gracias!
-¿Cómo te llamas?
-Me llamo Juan, ¿y Ud. cómo se llama?
-Me llamo Laura.

-¿De dònde eres?
-Soy de Estados Unidos. ¿y tú?
-Soy de México.
-¿Cuántos años tienes?
- Tengo 30 años.
-¿Y dónde vives?
-Vivo cerca del mar en Puerta Vallarta. ¿Y tú?

-Vivo en las montañas.
-¡Que bueno! Es un placer.
-¡El placer es mío!
-Good evening friend!
-Hello! How are you?
-Really good, thanks, ¿And you?
-Wonderful, thank you so much!
-What is your name?
-My name is Juan, And what is your name?
-My name is Laura.

-Where are you from?
-I am from the U.S. And you?
-I am from Mexico.
-How old are you?
- I am 30 years old.
-Where do you live?
-I live near the sea in Puerta Vallarta. And you?
-I live in the mountains.
-That's good! It's a pleasure.
-The pleasure is mine!

Match the Phrases

1. Vivo en Alemania.	j. I live in Germany.
2. Mucho gusto.	i. Nice to meet you.
3. Soy José.	a. I am Joseph.
4. Vivo en el campo.	b. I live in the country.
5. Soy de Inglaterra.	g. I am from England.
6. Que tenga un buen día	e. Have a good day.
7. ¿Qué hay?	h. What's new
8. ¿Cómo le va?	c. How's it going?
9. Nos vemos	f. See you.
10. ¿Cómo se llama?	d. What's your name?

Describing your world

This section is dedicated to help you describe yourselves and the people and things around you. I will also include a section to help describe some emotions and conditions. Here are some phrases to help you describe that new beautiful word you will be visiting.

Phrases to describe each other

He is tall	Él es alto

She is short	Ella es baja
My cat is fat	Mi gato es gordo.
They are thin	Ellos son delgados.
They (all girls) are pretty	Ellas son bonitas
My boyfriend is handsome	Mi novio es guapo
You are cute.	Tú eres lindo/a
She has short hair	Ella tiene pelo corto.
Short (length)	Corto/a
He has long hair.	Él tiene pelo largo.
Long	Largo/a
Skinny	Flaco/a
Big	Grande
Small	Pequeño/a
Strong	Fuerte
Ugly	Feo/a
Old	Viejo/a
Young	Joven

¡Ojo! Don't forget that the adjectives have to match the nouns according to number and gender.

Ex:

Gata gorda = Fat cat = *April*

Perro delgado =Skinny dog = *Yemu.*

More Description Phrases and Vocabulary

What's it like?	¿Cómo es?
What does he/she look like?	¿Cómo es él/ella?
I am ...	Soy ...
What color is his/her hair?	¿De qué color es su pelo?
She is blonde	Ella es rubia.
...ave brown hair	Tengo el pelo castaño.
	Él es pelirrojo.
...n?	¿Ella es morena?
	Blanco/a
	Limpio/a
	Sucio/a
	Mojado/a

Dry	Seco/a

¡**Ojo!** Remember Spanish speakers often add **'ito'** to the end of an adjective (**morenito, blanquita, flaquito**) to make it cute, emphasize, or sometimes for no reason at all!

Culture Note- It is very common in Spanish-speaking cultures to call people names using adjectives. For example, they will say, Hey skinny guy, fat man, youngin', old man, tall man (**Eh flaco, gordo, joven, viejo, grande**). Is she the skinny, dark-skinned, or fair-skinned one? (**¿Ella es la flaquita, morenita, o blanquita?**). The diminutive 'ito' can be used for both males and females.

¡Los Ejercicios!

Translate the phrases to English.

1. Ellas son bonitas y jovenes.   -

_____

2. Él tiene el pelo corto.   -

_____

3. ¿Tu novio es guapo?   -

_____

4. Ellos son feos.   -

_____

5. Tengo el pelo rubio.   -

_____

Find the correct sentence for each group and translate.

1.
____ Ella es morena.
____ Ella es moreno.
____ Él es morena.

_____

2.
____ Mis amigos son flacas.
____ Mis amigas son flacos
____ Mis amigos son flacos.

_____

3.

_____ El perro está sucio.

_____ El perro está sucia

_____ Los perros está sucio

4.

_____ Nosotros somos bajas.

_____ Nosotros somos bajo

_____ Nosotros somos bajos

Match the Vocabulary

1. viejo   a. short
2. largo   b. small
3. pequeño   c. old
4. pelirrojo   d. dry
5. limpia   e. pretty
6. mojado   f. wet
7. seco   g. clean
8. blanco   h. redhead
9. bonita   i. white
10. corto   j. long

*Below I will list some words to describe your emotions. You should use forms of the verb *estar* to talk about your emotions. Review the conjugations of 'estar' in the Grammar section.

Ex:

estoy emocionada. = I am excited.

How ya feeling?

How do you feel?	¿Cómo te sientes?
I feel good today.	Me siento bien hoy.
I'm happy	Estoy felíz or contento/a
What's a matter?	¿Qué te pasa?
I'm sad.	Estoy triste.
I'm a little tired.	Estoy un poco cansado/a
I'm so excited!	Estoy muy emocionado/a.

I'm somewhat bored.	Estoy más o menos aburrido/a.
I'm pretty angry.	Estoy bastante enojado/a
Angry/Upset	Molesto/a
Are you nervous	¿Está nervioso/a?
I feel calm/relaxed.	Me siento tranquilo/a.
I have been so busy!	¡He estado muy ocupado/a!
Scared	Asustado/a
I am scared of...	Tengo miedo de...
Heights	Las Alturas
The dark	La Oscuridad
Spiders	Las arañas
Snakes	Los serpientes/Las culebras
Rats	Las ratas

Translate the sentence.

1. Yo estoy muy tranquilo.   -

_____

2. Tengo miedo de la oscuridad. .   -

_____

3. ¿Tú estás ocupado?   -

_____

4. Ella está molesta.   -

_____

5. Nosotros estamos emocionados. -

_____

Match the Vocabulary

1. Las arañas   a. bored

2. Tengo miedo de   b. happy
3. Cansada   c. heights
4. Triste   d. scared

5. Enojado   e. nervous

6. Aburrida   f. spiders

7. Las alturas   g. angry

8. Asustado   h. sad
9. Feliz   i. I'm scared of...

10. Nerviosa   j. tired

Phrases using 'Tener'

Below are some phrases using the verb 'tener' to describe various emotions and conditions. Remember how to say how old you are? 'Tengo 30 años – I have 30 years.' So you already know one 'tener' expression. 'Tener' normally means 'to have' but is translated to 'to be' with these particular expressions.

Expressions using 'Tener'

Tengo hambre	I am hungry
¿Tienes sed?	Are you thirsty?
Tener frío	To be cold.
Tengo calor.	I am hot.
Tenemos sueño.	We are sleepy.
¿Tienes miedo?	Are you scared?
Ella tiene razón.	She is right.
Tener cuidado	To be careful
¡Ten cuidado!	Be careful!
Él tiene éxito.	He is successful.

Translate to English

1. Tengo mucho miedo.

_____

2. ¿Tienes sueño?

_____

3. Tenemos frío.

_____

4. ¿Tienes calor?

_____

5. Tengo hambre.

_____

Describing your World Answers

Translate the phrases to English.

1. Ellas son bonitas y jovenes.   <u>They are pretty and young.</u>
2. Él tiene el pelo corto.   <u>He has short hair.</u>
3. ¿Tu novio es guapo?   <u>Is your boyfriend handsome?</u>
4. Ellos son feos.   <u>They are ugly.</u>
5. Tengo el pelo rubio.   <u>I have blonde hair.</u>

Find the correct sentence for each group and translate

1.
<u>x</u> Ella es morena.
____ Ella es moreno.
____ Él es morena.   <u>She has dark skin</u>

2.
____ Mis amigos son flacas.
____ Mis amigas son flacos
x Mis amigos son flacos.   <u>My friends are skinny.</u>

3.
<u>x</u> El perro está sucio.
____ El perro está sucia
____ Los perros está sucio   <u>The dog is dirty.</u>

4.
____ Nosotros somos bajas.
____ Nosotros somos bajo
x Nosotros somos bajos   <u>We are short.</u>

Match the Vocabulary

1. viejo   c. old

2. Largo   j. long
3. Pequeño   b. small

4. Pelirrojo   h. redhead

5. Limpia   g. clean

6. Mojado   f. wet

7. Seco   d. dry

8. Blanco   i. white
9. Bonita   e. pretty
10. Corto   a. short

Translate the sentence.

1. Yo estoy muy tranquilo.   I am very calm.
2. Tengo miedo de la oscuridad. .   I am afraid of the dark.
3. ¿Tú estás ocupado?   Are you busy?
4. Ella está molesta.   She is upset.
5. Nosotros estamos emocionados.   We are excited.

Match the Vocabulary

1. Las arañas   f. spiders
2. Tengo miedo de   i. I'm scared of...
3. Cansada   j. tired
4. Triste   h. sad

5. Enojado   g. angry

6. Aburrida   a. bored

7. Las alturas   c. heights

8. Asustado   d. scared
9. Feliz   b. happy
10. Nerviosa   e. nervous

Translate to English

1. Tengo mucho miedo.   I am very scared.

2. ¿Tienes sueño?	<u>Are you sleepy?</u>
3. Tenemos frío.	<u>We are cold.</u>
4. ¿Tienes calor?	<u>Are you hot?</u>
5. Tengo hambre.	<u>I am hungry.</u>

Occupations

Now that we are able to greet, introduce, and describe ourselves, we can talk about what we do, our career. It is something that we often talk about and that sometimes, unfortunately, can consume our lives. In Latin American culture, they are often surprised at how work is such a big part of our lives. Helping each other out as friends and family is often more important than one's individual career and success. Also, many times, nepotism can be prevalent in Spanish-speaking countries. You will find that people do business with family or those that they know and are comfortable with. People also often prefer to do business in person rather than making phone calls or emailing. In this chapter, you will learn phrases to talk about some of the basic professions of our society.

Career Vocabulary

What do you do/What does s/he do?	¿En qué trabaja Ud./él/ella?
I am a teacher.	Soy profesora/a.
Ella es una actríz.	She is an actress.
Businessman/Business woman	Empresario/Empresaria
Is he a nurse?	Él es un enfermero
Are you a lawyer?	¿Usted es abogado/abogada?
They are writers.	Ellos son escritores.
There is the police.	Allí está la policia.
I am a firefighter.	Soy bombero/bombera.
Is she a student?	¿Ella es una estudiante?
I work in an office.	Trabajo en una oficina.
Actor/Actress	Actor/Actríz
Ambassador	Embajador/a
Architect	Arquitecto/a
Artist	Artista
Cook	Cocinero/Cocinera
Dentist	Dentista
Doctor	Medico/Médica or Doctor /Doctora

Driver	Conductor/Conductora
Electrician	Electricista
Engineer	Ingeniero/Ingeniera
Minister	Pastor
Model	Modelo
Musician	Músico
Pilot	Piloto/a
Receptionist	Recepcionista
Salesperson	Vendedor/Vendedora
Serviceman/woman	Militar
Social worker	Trabajador/a Social
Waiter	Mesero/Mesera

¡Ojo! Why are there two ways to say some of the professions, for example, **mesero** and **mesera**? One is referring to males and one to females. Some professions are the same for both males and females, like **Dentista**. Only the articles change, **un dentist** = a male dentist and **una dentista** = a female dentist

¡Los Ejercicios!

Answer the questions in a complete sentence based on the parentheses.

1. ¿En que trabaja ella? -

_____(servicewo man).

2. ¿En que trabaja él?

_____ (ambassador).

3. ¿En que trabajan ellas?

_____ (architects).

4. ¿En que trabajan ellos?

_____ (drivers).

5. ¿En que trabajas tú?

_____(Answer based on your

profession)

Unscramble and Translate

1. ícplioa   _____

2. diémoc   _____

3. tsproa   _____

4. maaorebjd   _____

5. obrombe   _____

6. mfneorre   _____

7. apmeoiersr   _____

8. ddeervona   _____

9. tpaoli   _____

10. oagodba   _____

Occupations Answers

Answer the questions in a complete sentence based on the parentheses.

1. ¿En que trabaja ella?   Ella es una militar.   (servicewoman).
2. ¿En que trabaja él?   Él es un embajador.   (ambassador).
3. ¿En que trabajan ellas?   Ellas son arquitectas   (architects).
4. ¿En que trabajan ellos?   Ellos son conductores.   (drivers).
5. ¿En que trabajas tú?   Answers will vary _____
(Answer based on your profession)

Unscramble and Translate

1. ícplioa   policía - police
2. diémoc   medico - doctor

3. tsproa   pastor - minister

4. maaorebjd   embajador -ambassador

5. obrombe	bombero - firefighter
6. mfneorre	enfermero - nurse
7. apmeoiersr	empresario – businessman
8. ddeervona	vendedora - saleswoman
9. tpaoli	pilota - pilot
10. oagodba	abogado - lawyer

Interests

Now that we have learned how to describe yourself, your family, and occupation, we can move onto discussing what you enjoy doing in your free time. Below you will find useful phrases to discuss our hobbies and interests.

Tiempo Libre (Free Time)

What do you like to do in your free time? (formal)	¿Qué **le** gusta hacer en su tiempo libre?
What do you like to do in your free time? (informal)	¿Qué **te** gusta hacer en tu tiempo libre?
I like to exercise.	Me gusta hacer ejercicios.
I don't like to play videogames.	No me gusta jugar videojuegos.
Do you like to travel?	¿Te gusta viajar?
I really like reading novels	Me gusta mucho leer novelas.
Do you want to go to the beach?	¿Quiere ir a la playa?
Do you play sports?	¿Juega deportes?
Do you watch TV much?	¿Ves la televisión mucho?
We watch a lot of sports.	Vemos muchos deportes.
I love listening to music	Me encanta escuchar música
Do you play an instrument?	¿Toca un instrumento?
He/She likes to write.	(A él/a ella) le gusta escribir.
Do you want to hang out?	¿Quieres pasar tiempo conmigo?

*Review the use of the verb *'gustar'* in the Grammar section in the Introduction.

¡Los Ejercicios!

Fill in the blank with the correct word and then translate sentence to English.

música	novelas	instrumento
conmigo	viajar	escribir

1. Me gusta escuchar _____.

_____

2. ¿Uds. tocan un _____?

_____

3. ¿Quieres pasar tiempo _____?

_____

4. Nos gusta _____ a España.

_____

5. A ella le gusta _____ libros.

_____

Match the Sentences

1. Te gusta leer novelas.   a. He loves to play
videogames.

2. Nos gusta hacer ejercicios.   b. I don't like to go to the
beach.

3. Me gusta ver muchos deportes.   c. We like to exercise.

4. A él le encanta jugar videojuegos.   d. Do you like to read
novels?

5. No me gusta ir a la playa.   e. I like to watch lots of
sports.

Interests Answers

Fill in the blank with the correct word and then translate sentence to English.

1. Me gusta escuchar <u>música</u>.   <u>I like to listen to music.</u>
2. ¿Uds. tocan un <u>instrumento</u>?   <u>Do you all play an instrument?</u>
3. ¿Quieres pasar tiempo <u>conmigo</u>?   <u>Do you want to hang out with me?</u>
4. Nos gusta <u>viajar</u> a España.   <u>We like to travel to Spain.</u>
5. A ella le gusta <u>escribir</u> libros.   <u>She likes to write books.</u>

Match the Sentences

1. ¿Te gusta leer novelas?   d. Do you like to read novels?

2. Nos gusta hacer ejercicios.   c. We like to exercise.

3. Me gusta ver muchos deportes.   e. I like to watch lots of sports.

4. A él le encanta jugar videojuegos.   a. He loves to play
videogames.

5. No me gusta ir a la playa.   b. I don't like to go to the beach.

Family Matters

This section is dedicated to talking about *la familia*. Family is the number one priority for the people of Latin America as I have mentioned. In our culture, we are typically more focused on individual success and enjoyment. In Spanish speaking countries, family and group achievement are most important. On a vacation, people are more likely to spend time with family than to go out with friends indicating their obligation to the family. You also are more likely to see extended family living with each other, nieces and nephews living with their aunts and uncles, and grandparents living with their children, etc. It even seems like neighbors and close friends are treated like family. In our culture, independence is valued and in theirs interdependence. When you are down, I help you up, and when I am down, you help me up. Observing this virtuous quality in Latin America has made me wish we were a little more like that. Understanding this family dynamic will help you to further understand their culture. Below I have provided you with phrases to talk about family.

Vocabulario de la Familia (Family Vocabulary)

Family values	Los Valores Familiares
Family meal	La Comida Familiar
Brother	Hermano
Sister	Hermana
Mom	Mamá
Dad	Papá
Mother	Madre
Father	Padre
Grandpa/Grandma	Abuelo/Abuela
Grandchildren	Los nietos
Grandson	El nieto
Granddaughter	La nieta
Cousin (female/male)	Primo/Prima
Husband/Wife	Esposo/Esposa
Son/Daughter	Hijo/Hija
Uncle/Aunt	Tío/Tía
Nephew/Niece	Sobrino/Sobrina
Mother-in-law	Suegra
Father-in-law	Suegro
Sister-in-law	Cuñada
Brother-in-law	Cuñado
Daughter-in-law	Nuera
Son-in-law	Yerno

¡Ojo! Notice again how Spanish differentiates between females and males more frequently.   With the word 'cousin' in English you don't immediately know if it is a male or female cousin. In Spanish you know for sure (**primo or prima**).

Phrases to talk about your immediate Family

How many siblings do you have?	¿Cúantos hermanos tiene?
There are five of us.	Somos cinco.
I have two brothers.	Tengo dos hermanos.
He has 3 sisters and one brother.	Él tiene tres hermanas y un hermano.
I have one older brother.	Tengo un hermano mayor.
She has one younger sister.	Ella tiene una hermana menor.
¿Do you have any children?	¿Ud. tiene hijos?
I have one son and two daughters.	Tengo un hijo y dos hijas.
How old are they?	¿Cuántos años tienen?

My son is 20, one daughter is 18, and the other is 15.	Mi hijo tiene veinte, una hija tiene dieciocho, y la otra tiene quince.
What do your parents do?	¿En qué trabajan sus padres?
My dad is a teacher and my mom is a nurse.	Mi papá es profesor y mi mamá es enfermera.

Phrases to talk about Extended Family

Are all of your grandparents alive?	Todos sus abuelos están vivos?
One grandpa has passed away.	Un abuelo ha fallecido.
How many cousins do you have?	¿Cuántos primos tiene Ud.?
There are 10 of us.	Somos diez.
I am a twin.	Soy una melliza/un mellizo.
They are identical twins.	Ellos/ellas son gemelos/gemelas.
Do you like your mother-in-law?	¿Le agrada su suegra?
My parents are divorced.	Mis padres están divorciados.
I have a stepmom/stepdad	Tengo una madrastra/padrastro.
I have a stepsister/stepbrother	Tengo una hermanastra/hermanastro.
Stepchild	Hijastro/a
I am adopted.	Estoy adoptado/adoptada.
Madrina	Godmother
Padrino	Godfather
Do you have a pet?	¿Ud. tiene una mascota?
We have a dog and cat.	Tenemos un perro y un gato.
I have a fish and a bird.	Tengo un pez y un pájaro.

*In Spanish-speaking cultures the relationship between godparents and their godchildren is typically much closer than what we are used to.

*Review conjugations of the verb 'Tener' in the grammar section of the Introduction.

¡Los Ejercicios!

Translate the sentences to English.

1. Yo tengo cuatro abuelos.   -

_____

2. Tengo una hermana mayor.   -

_____

3. Mi abuela ha fallecido   -

_____

4. ¿Tienes una mascota?   -

_____

5. ¿En qué trabajan tus padres?   -

_____

Translate the sentences to Spanish.

1. Are all of your grandparents alive?   -

_____

2. They are twins.   -

_____

3. I have a stepmom.

_____

4. They are six of us.   -

_____

5. I have a fish and a bird.   -

_____

Unscramble and Translate

1. tesino   _____

2. ornoibs   _____

3. aredp   _____

4. emnhrao   _____

5. oaucñd   _____

6. luaoeb   _____

7. urena   _____

8. oryen   _____

9. arsamdatr   _____

10. arnopdi   _____

Family Matters Answers

Translate the sentences to English.

1. Yo tengo cuatro abuelos.   I have four grandparents.
2. Tengo una hermana mayor.   I have an older sister.
3. Mi abuela ha fallecido   My grandma has passed away.
4. ¿Tienes una mascota?   Do you have a pet?
5. ¿En qué trabajan tus padres?   What do your parents do (job)?

Translate the sentences to Spanish.

1. Are all of your grandparents alive?   ¿Todos tus abuelos están vivos?
2. They are twins.   Ellos son gemelos or gemelas.
3. I have a stepmom.   Tengo una madrastra.
4. They are six of us.   Somos seis.
5. I have a fish and a bird.   Tengo un pez y un pájaro.

Unscramble and Translate

1. tesino   nietos-grandchildren

2. ornoibs   sobrino - nephew

3. aredp   padre - father

4. emnhrao   hermano - brother

5. oaucñd   cuñado – brother–in-law

6. luaoeb   abuelo - grandpa

7. urena   nuera – daughter–in-law

8. oryen   yerno – son-in-law

9. arsamdatr   madrastra - stepmother

10. arnopdi   <u>padrino - godfather</u>

Think about how you would describe your family in Spanish.

Ex: Yo tengo dos hermanos menores y una hermana mayor. Mi mama es una profesora y mi papa es un enfermero. Mis padres están divorciados. Tengo ocho primos. Tres son primas y cinco son primos. Mis cuatro abuelos están vivos. Tengo dos mascotas, una gata y un perro.

Now you try!

Chapter 4
Having Fun in the City (Shopping, Dining, Nightlife)

Now that we have gotten around the city, found a place to stay and made some *amigos*. Let's see if we can go out and have some fun with them! The first part of this chapter helps you to find a bargain while shopping around. The second part will discuss cuisine and going out to eat. The one that follows will teach you about nightlife and dating whether you prefer to go clubbing, barhopping, or to house parties. The fourth section will teach you a little culture by helping you to get around museums along with a variety of other cultural destinations. In the last part, you will learn about sports and outdoor activities.

-Shopping

- Bonus: Size Conversation Chart

-Wining and Dining

-Nightlife and Dating

-Cultural visits and activities

-Sports and Outdoors

Shopping Around

This section will help you to avoid getting cheated even though the vender sees the *gringo* or *gringa* coming a mile away. Show him or her that you do know your stuff by using the phrases in this chapter. Remember that outside of major cities, many times shops will be closed in the afternoon from around 2 to 5. The owners will often go home to *almorzar* (have lunch) and have a *siesta* (nap) Take advantage and use this time to rest, especially to prepare for the Spanish nightlife that you will learn about soon! Here are some phrases to help you find that perfect gift for your Mom or little keepsake to never forget your trip.

¿Dónde y cómo ir de compras? (Where and how to shop)

Clothing store	La tienda de ropa
Shopping mall	El centro commercial/El mall

What time do you open?	¿A qué hora abren?
What time do you close?	¿A qué hora cierran?
salesman/saleswoman	El vendedor/la vendedora
Do you accept credit cards?	¿Acepta tarjetas de crédito?
We only accept cash.	Sólo aceptamos efectivo.
Fitting room	Probador
Can I try it on?	¿Puedo probármelo?
It's too small.	Está pequeño.
It's too big.	Está grande.
Do you have any bigger/smaller?	¿Tiene más grande/más pequeño?

Más frases de compras (More shopping phrases)

How can I help you?	¿Cómo le puedo ayudar?
How much does it cost?	¿Cuánto cuesta?
How much is it?	¿Cuánto es?
Which one do you want?	¿Cuál quiere?
What size?	¿Qué tamaño?/¿Qué talla?
I would like that one.	Quisiera ese (masculine) esa (feminine)
It's too expensive	Está muy caro
Do you have...?	¿Tiene ...?
I'm just looking.	Sólo estoy mirando.
Of course!	¡Claro que sí!
Is there a sale?	¿Hay alguna oferta?

¡Los Ejercicios!

Match the Vocabulary

1. ¿Acepta tarjetas de crédito?   a. It's too small.
2. ¿Puedo probármelo?   b. We only accept
cash.
3. Está pequeño.   c. Can I try it on?
4. ¿Tiene más grande?   d. Do you accept
credit cards?
5. Sólo aceptamos efectivo.   e. Do you have any
bigger?

Translate to Spanish

1. How can I help you?

   _____

2. I would like that one.

   _____

3. I'm just looking.

   _____

4. Are there any sales?

   _____

5. How much does it cost?

   _____

La Ropa de Damas (Women's Clothing)

Dress	El vestido
Skirt	La falda
Blouse	La blusa
Jeans	Los jeans
Tights	Las medias
High Heels	Tacones
Bra	El sostén
Panties	Los calzones
Thong	La tanga

La Ropa de Caballeros (Men's Clothing)

Suit	El traje
Shirt	La camisa
Pants	Los pantalones
Tie	La corbata
Bowtie	La corbata de moño
Socks	Los calcetines
Shoes	Los zapatos
Sneakers	Los tenis

Unscramble and Translate

1. aubsl   _____

2. oaasztp   _____

3. ieasdm   _____
4. cceeinstla   _____

5. snctaoe   _____

6. aaorbct   _____

7. aaimsc   _____

8. jrtae   _____

9. snzacloe   _____

10. dlaaf   _____

La Ropa de Invierno (Winter Clothing)

Coat	El abrigo
Raincoat	El permeable
Boots	Las Botas
Gloves	Los guantes
Jacket	La chaqueta
Sweater	El sueter
Slippers	Las pantuflas
Hat	La gorra
Scarf	La bufanda

La Ropa de Verano (Summer Clothing)

Shorts	Los pantalones cortos/Los shorts
T-shirt	La camiseta
Swimsuit	El traje de baño
Flip flops	Las chancletas
Sunglasses	Los lentes del sol

Hat	El sombrero
Beach towel	La toalla de baño

Compras para la Casa (Shopping for the home)

I am looking for a comforter.	Busco un cubrecama.
I need a blue rug/carpet	Necesito una alfombra azul
Where are the...?	¿Dónde están ...?
Mirrors	Los espejos
Furniture	Los muebles
Lamps	Las lámparas
Dishes	Los platos
Sheets	Las sábanas
Pillows	Las almohadas

Match the Vocabulary

1. El abrigo   a. pillows

2. Las sábanas   b. mirrors
3. Las almohadas   c. flip-flops
4. Los lentes del sol   d. jacket
5. Los espejos   e. hat

6. Los muebles   f. coat
7. Las chancletas   g. swimsuit

8. La chaqueta   h. sunglasses
9. El traje de baño   i. sheets

10. La gorra   j. furniture

Shopping Around Answers

Match the Vocabulary

1. ¿Acepta tarjetas de crédito?   d. Do you accept credit cards?

2. ¿Puedo probármelo?   c. Can I try it on?

3. Está pequeño.   a. It's too small.
4. ¿Tiene más grande?   e. Do you have any bigger?
5. Sólo aceptamos efectivo.   b. We only accept cash.

Translate to Spanish
1. How can I help you?   ¿Cómo le puedo ayudar?
2. I would like that one.   Me gustaría ese/esa.
3. I'm just looking.   Sólo estoy mirando.
4. Are there any sales?   ¿Hay alguna oferta?
5. How much does it cost?   ¿Cuánto cuesta?

Unscramble and Translate

1. aubsl   blusa - blouse
2. oaasztp   zapatos - shoes

3. ieasdm   medias - tights
4. cceeinstla   calcetines - socks

5. snctaoe   tacones - highheels

6. aaorbct   corbata – necktie

7. aaimsc   camisa - shirt

8. jrtae   traje - suit

9. snzacloe   calzones - underwear

10. dlaaf   falda – skirt

Match the Vocabulary

1. El abrigo   f. coat

2. Las sábanas   i. sheets
3. Las almohadas   a. pillows
4. Los lentes del sol   h. sunglasses
5. Los espejos   b. mirrors

6. Los muebles	j. furniture
7. Las chancletas	c. flip-flops
8. La chaqueta	d. jacket
9. El traje de baño	g. swimsuit
10. La gorra	e. hat

Bonus: Size Conversion Chart

Below, I will convert U.S. sizes to the sizes used in Spain. In some cases they are the same sizes used in continental Europe.

Women's Clothing Sizes

U.S.	Spain
6	34
8	36
10	38
12	40
14	42
16	44
18	46
20	48

Women's Shoe Sizes

U.S.	Spain
4.5	36
5.5.	37
6.5	38
7.5	39
8.5	40
9.5	41
10.5	42
11.5	43

Men's Clothing Sizes

U.S.	Spain
34	44
36	46
38	48
40	50
42	52
44	54

Men's Shoe Sizes

U.S.	Spain
6.5	40
7.5	41
8.5	42
9.5	43
10.5	44
11.5	45
12.5	46

Children's Clothing Sizes

U.S.	Spain height cm
4	125
6	135
8	150
10	155
12	160
14	165

Wining and Dining

In this section we will help you to get a table, order, and do other restaurant-related tasks. You should know that in Spain times for eating are a bit different than what we would expect. Lunch is usually after 1:30 and for dinner often no earlier than 9pm. On the weekend dining out can start as late as 10pm. This is also true in many countries in Latin America. Also there are three main types of eateries: a restaurant which tends to be more formal, a bar which serves food and alcohol, and cafeteria which is kind of like a mixture between a bar, coffee shop and a bakery. In Spain, you can usually go to a *cafetería* (café) to have a *merienda* (snack) around 5:30 or 6:00pm. The world famous *Tapas* (small dishes served with a drink) are served at bars and cafeterías. In Spanish-speaking countries, it is also polite to use a knife and fork to eat almost anything. It is not normally accepted to eat food with your hands*.* *¡Buen provecho!* (Bon Apetit!)

Reservando una Mesa (Reserving a Table)

Hello, I'd like to reserve a table for Saturday night.	Hola, me gustaría reservar una mesa para la noche del sábado.
For how many?	¿Para cuántas personas?
For four people	Para cuatro personas.
At what time?	¿A qué hora?
At 9 pm	A las nueve de la noche.
What is the name for the reservation?	¿A nombre de quién está la reserva?
Would you like a seat inside or outside?	¿Le gustaría sentar adentro o afuera?
Is this table okay?	¿Le agrada esta mesa?
The restaurant is full tonight.	El restaurante está lleno esta noche.
There is a 30 minute wait.	Hay una espera de treinta minutos.
The restaurant holds a private party tonight.	Esta noche el restaurante tiene una fiesta privada.

(Pidiendo la comida) Ordering

Are you ready to order?	¿Están listos para pedir?
What would you like to drink	¿Qué le gustaría beber?
I would like to drink...	Me gustaría beber...
What starter would you like?	¿Cuál aperitivo le gustaría?
I would like ...	Quisiera ...
What tapas do you have today?	¿Qué son las tapas de hoy?
What are your specials today?	¿Qué son las ofertas de hoy?
Menu, please	El menú, por favor
What do you recommend?	¿Qué me recomienda?
Excuse me, sir/ma'am/miss	Perdón, señor /señora/señorita

Anything else?	¿Algo más?
Can you bring us/me…please?	Nos/me puede traer…por favor?
Napkins	Servilletas
Some more bread	Más pan
Another drink (alcoholic)	Otro trago
Another drink (non-alcoholic)	Otra bebida
More water	Más agua
Another glass of wine	Otro vaso de vino
Flatware	Los cubiertos
A fork	Un tenedor
A spoon	Una cuchara
A knife	Un cuchillo
An extra plate	Un plato extra
Would you like dessert…?	¿Le gustaría un postre?

¡Los Ejercicios!

Translate to English

1. ¿Le gustaría sentar adentro o afuera?

_____

2. ¿A nombre de quién está la reserva?

_____

3. El restaurante está lleno esta noche.

_____

4. ¿Le agrada esta mesa?

_____

5. Hay una espera de treinta minutos.

_____

Translate to Spanish

1. I would like to drink a glass of wine.

_____

2. Can you bring us napkins please?

_____

3. Can you bring me another drink?

_____

4. I would like more bread.

_____

5. What do you recommend?

_____

Food preferences

I'm a vegetarian.	Soy vegetariano/a.
What is the fish of the day?	¿Cuál es el pescado de hoy?
Do you serve breakfast all day?	¿Sirven desayuno todo el día?
Can you pass the…?	¿Me puede pasar…?
Can we share…?	¿Podemos compartir?
What does this dish have?	¿Qué tiene este plato?
Does this dish have…?	¿Este plato tiene…?
I'm allergic to…	Tengo alergia a…
Nuts	Nueces
Milk	Leche
Shellfish	Mariscos
Eggs	Huevos
Wheat	El trigo
Soy	La soya

More Food Vocabulary

Lunch	El almuerzo
Dinner	La cena
Meat	Carne
Chicken	Pollo
Ham	Jamón
Turkey	Pavo
Lamb	Cordero
Pasta	Pasta
Salad	Ensalada
Cheese	Queso
Vegetables	Verduras
A straw	Una pajita/Un sorbete
Soft Drink	Refresco
Juice	Jugo
A beer	Una cerveza

Dessert	El postre
Tip	La propina
The bill, please	La cuenta, por favor
I think there is an error in the bill.	Creo que hay un error en la cuenta.
Bon apetit!	¡Buen provecho!
Enjoy your meal!	¡Que aproveche!

¡Los Ejercicios!

Match the Vocabulary

1. El desayuno   a. fish
2. Buen provecho   b. dinner
3. Carne   c. vegetables
4. Queso   d. cheese

5. Verduras   e. breakfast
6. Pescado   f. soft drink

7. Refresco   g. Enjoy your meal.

8. El almuerzo   h. milk
9. La cena   i. lunch
10. Leche   j. meat

Translate the phrases

1. I'm a vegetarian.   _____
2. Can you pass me the salad?   _____
3. Can we share the pasta?   _____

Wining and Dining Answers

Translate to English

1. ¿Le gustaría sentar adentro o afuera?   <u>Would you like to sit inside</u>
<u>or outside?</u>

2. ¿A nombre de quién está la reserva?   <u>Whose name is the</u>
<u>reservation in?</u>

3. El restaurante está lleno esta noche.   The restaurant is full
tonight.

4. ¿Le agrada esta mesa?   Is this table okay?

5. Hay una espera de treinta minutos.   There is a 30 minute
wait.

Translate to Spanish

1. I would like to drink a glass of wine.   Me gustaría beber un vaso
de vino.

2. Can you bring us napkins please?   ¿Nos puede traer servilletas por
favor?

3. Can you bring me another drink?   ¿Me puede traer otro trago/otra
bebida?

4. I would like more bread.   Quisiera más pan.

5. What do you recommend?   ¿Qué me recomienda?

Match the Vocabulary

1. El desayuno   e. breakfast
2. Buen provecho   g. Enjoy your meal.
3. Carne   j. meat
4. Queso   d. cheese

5. Verduras   c. vegetables
6. Pescado   a. fish
7. Refresco   f. soft drink
8. El almuerzo   i. lunch
9. La cena   b. dinner
10. Leche   h. milk

Translate the phrases

1. I'm a vegetarian.	<u>Soy un/una vegetariana.</u>
2. Can you pass me the salad?	<u>¿Me puede pasar la</u> <u>ensalada?</u>
3. Can we share the pasta?	<u>Podemos compartir la pasta.</u>

Nightlife and Dating

This section will help you to enjoy the colorful nightlife and to make your way around the dating scene in your Spanish-speaking country. Similar to the schedule of eating, the timeline for going out is quite different. This is where you realize that taking that afternoon *siesta* is essential since people will not go out until after midnight and can stay out until sunrise. Also, make sure to pace yourself and eat *tapas* with your alcoholic drinks so you can keep up with your new Spanish-speaking friends during those marathon fiestas. Here are some phrases to help you in the dating scene and while going out to that bar, pub, club or whatever your favorite place to fiesta is.

Nightlife phrases

I feel like…	Tengo ganas de…
going to a party	ir a una fiesta
going to a bar	ir a un bar
going to a club	ir a una discoteca
going out with friends	salir con amigos
partying tonight	festejar esta noche
having a good time	pasarlo bien
going dancing	salir a bailar
tapear	go to various bars to order drinks and tapas.

Let's … (Vamos a…)

Get a drink.	Tomar un trago.
Eat at a restaurant.	Comer en un restaurante.
Eat out.	Salir a comer.
Go to the movies.	Ir al cine.
Watch a scary movie.	Ver una película de horror

Watch a comedy.	Ver una comedia.
Watch a chick flic.	Ver una comedia romántica.
Watch a mystery.	Ver una película de suspenso.
Have a party at my house.	Tener una fiesta en mi casa.
Go listen to live music.	Ir a escuchar música en vivo.
Are there subtitles for this movie?	¿Hay subtítulos para esta película?

Vamos a tomar un trago (Let's have a drink)

Let's cheer	Brindemos
Cheers!	¡Salud!
Let's celebrate	Celebremos
Like bottoms up (Literally up, down, to the middle, and inside)	Pa' arriba pa' abajo pa' centro y pa' dentro (When saying this you put your drink up, down, in the middle, and then drink it!)

Él/Ella (He/she...)

is drunk	está borracho/a
is tipsy	está mareado/a
is wasted	está embriagado/a
had too many drinks	tomó demasiado/a
is a happy drinker	es felíz cuando toma
is a sad drinker	es triste cuando toma
is an angry drunk	se enoja cuando toma
is hung over	está con la resaca

¡Los Ejercicios!

Match the Phrases

1. Pasarla bien.   a. to have a good time.
2. Salir a bailar   b. to go to a club
3. Festejar la noche.   c. to go to the movies.
4. Ir a una discoteca.   d. to party tonight
5. Ir al cine   e. to go out dancing

Fill in the blank with the word from the word bank and translate

película   resaca   tener

escuchar   borracho   dentro

1. Vamos a <u>tener</u> una fiesta en mi casa.

_____

2. ¿Hay subtítulos para esta <u>película</u>?

_____

3. Vamos a <u>escuchar</u> música en vivo.

_____

4. Pa' arriba pa' abajo pa' centro y pa' <u>dentro</u>.

_____

5. Ella está con la <u>resaca</u>.

_____

Choose the correct word from the parentheses.

1. Ella está_____(borracha/borracho).
2. Vamos a salir a _____ (comer/salud).
3. Él está _____ (mareada/mareado).
4. Vamos a tomar un _____ (cine/trago).
5. Vamos a ver una _____de horror. (película/fiesta).

Nightlife Answers

Match the Phrases

1. Pasarlo bien.   a. to have a good time.
2. Salir a bailar   e. to go out dancing
3. Festejar la noche.   d. to party tonight
4. Ir a una discoteca.   b. to go to a club
5. Ir al cine   c. to go to the movies.

Fill in the blank with the word from the word bank and translate

1. Vamos a <u>tener</u> una fiesta en mi casa------ <u>We are going to have a party in my house.</u>

2. ¿Hay subtítulos para esta <u>película</u>? ------ <u>Are there subtitles for this movie?</u>

3. Vamos a <u>escuchar</u> música en vivo. ------ <u>We are going to listen to live music.</u>

4. Pa' arriba pa' abajo pa' centro y pa' <u>dentro</u>. ------ <u>Up, down, in the middle, and inside.</u>

5. Ella está con la <u>resaca</u>. ------ <u>She is hungover.</u>

Choose the correct word from the parentheses.

1. Ella está <u>borracha </u>(borracha/borracho).
2. Vamos a salir a <u>comer</u> (comer/salud).
3. Él está <u>mareado</u> (mareada/mareado).
4. Vamos a tomar un <u>trago</u> (cine/trago).
5. Vamos a ver una <u>película </u>de horror. (película/fiesta).

Dating Scene

Are you alone?	¿Está solo/a Ud.?
Is anyone sitting here?	¿Alguien está sentado aquí?
May I sit next to you?	¿Puedo sentarme a su lado?
Of course!	¡Claro!
Can I buy you a drink?	¿Le puedo comprar un trago?
We know each other, right?	Nos conocemos, ¿verdad?
Do you want to go out with me?	¿Quieres salir conmigo?
Do you want to have dinner tonight?	¿Quieres cenar juntos esta noche?
You look beautiful! (woman)	¡Estás hermosa!
You look nice! (man)	¡Estás guapo!
I had a nice time with you.	Lo pasé muy bien contigo.
Can I have your phone number?	¿Me puede dar su número de teléfono?
Can I text you later?	¿Te puedo mandar un mensaje (de texto) más tarde?
Can I find you on facebook?	¿Te puedo buscar en facebook?
Sure!	¡Por supuesto!
Do you have a boyfriend/girlfriend?	¿Tienes novio/novia?
Are you married?	¿Estás casado/a?
I like you. (friendly)	Me caes bien.
I like you. (romantically)	Me gustas.
I love you.	Te quiero. (Not so serious)

| I love you. | Te amo. (More serious relationship) |
| I love you too. | Yo también te amo. |

¡El Rechazo! (Rejection!)

Thanks, but I'm expecting someone.	Gracias, pero estoy esperando a alguien.
Sorry, I'm not interested.	Perdón, no estoy interesado/a.
It's not gonna work out.	¡No va a funcionar!
You're not my type.	No eres mi tipo.
Stop calling me!	¡Deja de llamarme!
Please, leave me alone.	Por favor, déjeme en paz.
I have a boyfriend/girlfriend.	Tengo un novio/novia.
I am not looking for a boyfriend/girlfriend.	No busco novio/novia.
I just want to be friends.	Solo quiero ser amigos/as.
I don't like you.	Me caes mal.

¡Los Ejercicios!

Match the Vocabulary
1. ¿Quieres salir conmigo?
2. Me gustas
3. ¿Estás casado?
4. Te quiero

a. I like you.
b. I love you.
c. Are you married?
d. Stop calling me

5. Deja de llamarme.
6. No busco novio.
7. Estás hermosa.

e. You look nice.
f. I love you too.
g. Are you alone?

8. Yo también te amo

h. You look beautiful.

9. Estás guapo.

i. I'm not looking for a boyfriend

10. ¿Ud está solo?

j. Do you want to go out with me?

Translate to Spanish

1. Can I buy you a drink?

_____

2. Can I find you on facebook

_____

3. I had a nice time with you.

_____

4. Thanks, but I'm expecting someone.

_____

5. Please, leave me alone.

_____

Dating Scene Answers

Match the Vocabulary

1. ¿Quieres salir conmigo?	j. Do you want to go out with me?
2. Me gustas	a. I like you.
3. ¿Estás casado?	c. Are you married?
4. Te quiero	b. I love you.
5. Deja de llamarme.	d. Stop calling me
6. No busco novio.	i. I'm not looking for a boyfriend
7. Estás hermosa.	h. You look beautiful.
8. Yo también te amo	f. I love you too.
9. Estás guapo.	e. You look nice.
10. ¿Ud está solo?	g. Are you alone?

Translate to Spanish

1. Can I buy you a drink? ------ ¿Le puedo comprar un trago?

2. Can I find you on facebook ------¿Te puedo buscar en Facebook?

3. I had a nice time with you. ------ Lo pasé bien contigo.

4. Thanks, but I'm expecting someone. ------ Gracias, pero estoy esperando a alguien.

5. Please, leave me alone. ------ <u>Por favor, déjenme en paz.</u>

Cultural Visits and Activities

With so many world famous artists having called Spain home, it is no surprise that there are numerous world-renowned museums and art galleries to visit in the country. Latin America has its fair share of fascinating art galleries and history museums as well in part due to the captivating history of its countries. Most major museums in Spain are open from 9am to 7pm, Tuesday through Sunday. Some museums have one day a week in which entry is free, usually on Sundays. In Madrid and Barcelona, using their *Tarjeta de Descuento* (Discount Card) you can obtain free entry to museums, monuments, free travel on public transportation, discounts in shops, restaurants and theatres, and in Barcelona discount entry to museums, shows, and attractions. Because of the largely catholic population, Spain and Latin American countries are full of beautiful cathedrals. Occasionally entry is free, but there is often a fee for non-worshippers to pay. Remember to keep your clothing conservative to enter, making sure to cover your shoulders and legs. Here are some phrases to help you get a little culture while travelling in your Spanish-speaking country.

Me gustaría ir … (I would like to go…)

Visit a museum.	A visitar un museo.
Watch a play.	A ver una obra.
Go to the theater.	Al teatro.
Go to the opera.	A una ópera.
Go to a concert.	A un concierto.
A classical music concert.	A un concierto de música clásica.
A rock music concert.	A un concierto de música rock.
A jazz concert.	A un concierto de música jazz.
A puppet show.	A un espectáculo de marionetas.

Perdón, quisiera (Excuse me, I would like…)

To buy a ticket.	Comprar una entrada.
A guidebook.	Una guía.
To use my discount card.	Usar mi tarjeta de descuento.
To take photos with flash.	Sacar fotos con flash.
To go on a guided tour.	Hacer una gira con guía turístico.

One seat in the balcony.	Un asiento en el balcón.
A front row seat.	Un asiento de primera fila.

Necesito información. (I need some information.)

How much is the museum entrance ticket?	¿Cuánto cuesta la entrada para el museo?
The full price/half price ticket costs ten euros.	El precio completo/medio cuesta diez euros.
At what time will the English tour start?	¿A qué hora comienza la gira en inglés?
The tour in English will start in ten minutes.	La gira en inglés comienza en diez minutos.
At what time is the museum closed on Sundays?	¿A qué hora se cierra el museo los domingos?
Where is the bathroom?	¿Dónde está el baño?
Is there a souvenir shop?	¿Hay una tienda de souvenirs?
Where can I buy refreshments?	¿Dónde puedo comprar comida y bebida?

¡Los Ejercicios!

Match the Phrases

1. Quisiera ir al teatro.
2. Me gustaría ir a ver una obra.
3. ¿Te gustaría ir a un concierto?
concert?
4. Un asiento en el balcón.
5. Usar mi tarjeta de descuento
theater.

a. I would like to see a play.
b. One seat in the balcony.
c. Would you like to go to a

d. Use my discount card.
e. I would like to go the

Translate to English

Quisiera....

    1. Un asiento de primera fila.

_____

2. Comprar una entrada.

_____

3. Sacar fotos con flash.

_____

4. Ir a un espectáculo de marionetas.

_____

5. ir a una ópera.

_____

Cultural Visits and Activities Answers

Match the Phrases

1. Quisiera ir al teatro. ------ e. I would like to go the theater.
2. Me gustaría ir a ver una obra. ------ a. I would like to see a play.
3. ¿Te gustaría ir a un concierto. ------ c. Would you like to go to a concert?
4. Un asiento en el balcón------ b. One seat in the balcony.
5. Usar mi tarjeta de descuento------ d. Use my discount card.

Translate to English

Quisiera….   I would like

   1. Un asiento de primera fila. ------ a front row seat.
   2. Comprar una entrada. ------ to buy a ticket.
   3. Sacar fotos con flash. ------ to take flash photos.
   4. Ir a un espectáculo de marionetas------ to go to a puppet

show.

   5. ir a una ópera. ------ to go to an opera.

Sports and Outdoors

This section will help you to enjoy sports and other activities in the breathtaking landscapes of Spain and Latin America. Spanish-speaking countries have so much to offer in the realm of outdoor activities. Whether it be *esquiar* (skiing) los Andes in South America, scuba diving in the Caribbean, or hiking in the Spanish Pyrenees, you won't have a chance to get bored on your travels. Here are some phrases to help you find and Schedule some outdoor activities in Spanish.

Los Deportes (Sports)

Do you want to play... with me?	¿Quieres jugar... conmigo?
Basketball	Al basquetból
Soccer	Al futból
Football	Al futból americano
Tennis	Al tenís
Chess	Al ajedrez
Volleyball	Al voleiból
Golf	Al golf
Ping pong	Al tenis de mesa
Bowling	A los bolos

¡Ojo! There are two ways to say 'play' in Spanish. In order to say, 'to play a sport or other activity like 'chess' you say *'jugar al...'* In order to say 'to play an instrument, you say *'tocar...'*

Ex:

Jugar al voleiból = To play volleyball
Tocar la guitarra = To play the guitar

Ven conmigo a ...(Come with me to...)

A gym.	Un gimnasio.
An aerobics class.	Una clase de aeróbic.
A yoga class.	Una clase de yoga.
Exercise.	Hacer ejercicios
Go biking.	Andar en bicicleta.
Go hiking.	Hacer una caminata.
Go jogging.	Salir a trotar.
Go sailing.	Salir a navegar.
Go skiing.	Esquiar.
Go kayaking.	Andar en kayak.
Go surfing.	Surfear
Go skateboarding.	Andar en patineta.
Ride horses.	Montar en caballo.

Quisiera ir (I would like to go...)

Hunting.	A cazar.
Fishing.	A pescar.
The mountains.	A las montañas.
To the sea.	Al mar.
To the beach.	A la playa.
To the countryside.	Al campo.
Swimming	A nadar.
Camping.	De camping.
Scuba diving.	A bucear.
What are you going to do on the weekend?	¿Qué vas a hacer el fin de semana?
What are you going to do on the holiday?	¿Qué vas a hacer para el feriado?

¡Los Ejercicios!

Unscramble and Translate

1. lóvoevib   _____
 2. flog   _____

 3. sítne   _____

4. eerdjaz   _____
5. óbuft   _____

6. suareqi   _____
7. lbcloaa   _____
8. reucba   _____

9. aardn   _____
10. zcaa   _____

Match the Phrases

1. Quisiera ir al campo.   a. Come with me to ride horses.

2. ¿Te gustaría salir a navegar? b. I would like to go on a hike.
3. Ven conmigo a montar en caballo. c. Would you like to go sailing?
4. Quisiera hacer una camineta. d. I like to play table tennis.
5. Me gusta jugar al tenis de mesa. e. I would like to go to the countryside.

Translate to English

1. Voy a bucear en México.

   _____

2. Mi amiga y yo vamos a la playa.

   _____

3. Me gusta salir a trotar.

   _____

4. ¿Te gusta andar en bicicleta?

   _____

5. Ven conmigo a jugar al tenis.

   _____

Sports and Outdoors Answers

Unscramble and Translate

1. lóvoevib	voleiból - volleyball
2. flog	golf - golf
3. sítne	tenís - tennis
4. eerdjaz	ajedrez - chess
5. óbuft	futból - soccer
6. suareqi	esquiar – to ski
7. lbcloaa	caballo - horse
8. reucba	bucear – to scuba-dive

9. aardn   <u>nadar – to swim</u>

10. zcaar   <u>cazar – to hunt</u>

Match the Phrases

1. Quisiera ir al campo.   e. I would like to go to the
countryside.
2. ¿Te gustaría salir a navegar?   c. Would you like to go sailing?

3. Ven conmigo a montar en caballo.   a. Come with me to ride horses.
4. Quisiera hacer una camineta.   b. I would like to go on a hike.

5. Me gusta jugar al tenis de mesa.   d. I like to play table tennis.

Translate to English

1. Voy a bucear en México.   <u>I'm going to scuba dive in Mexico.</u>

2. Mi amiga y yo vamos a la playa. <u>My friend and I are going to the beach.</u>

3. Me gusta salir a trotar.   <u>I like to go jogging.</u>
4. ¿Te gusta andar en bicicleta?   <u>Do you like to go biking?</u>
5. Ven conmigo a jugar al tenis.   <u>Come with me to play tennis.</u>

Chapter 5
"Help Me Out, Please!"

This chapter is dedicated to those critical situations that we must be prepared for and the conversations we must have. I will include phrases to help you if you are sick or have another kind of emergency. It will also provide you with vocabulary to use in the bank, and to talk about the time and weather.

-Illnesses and Emergencies

-Money in the Bank

-Time will tell

-How's the Weather?

Illnesses and Emergencies

This chapter will help you to survive those minor illnesses and any other emergencies such as losing your passport, credit cards etc. Things that often seem to happen to us when we are abroad and out of our comfort zone. Being sick and/or in trouble is no fun and can be even worse in a foreign country, far away from family, friends, and familiarity. Being able to communicate a little more to the doctors or emergency personnel in their language will hopefully help. In Spain if you are sick and it is not too serious you can go to a **centro de salud** (public health center) or to see your **medico cabacero** (family doctor). The healthcare set up in other Spanish speaking countries will vary. You can always ask, **¿Dónde hay un Doctor?** (Where is there a Doctor?) and hope to find a local to help you out. Of course, if it is an emergency, go directly to a hospital. If your Doctor gives you a prescription, you will find pharmacies almost everywhere with a green cross on their sign. Be prepared to pay the Doctor **en efectivo** (in cash). Here are some phrases to help you survive those illnesses and emergencies.

Necesito... (I need...)

Eye drops	Las gotas para los ojos
Cough syrup	El jarabe para la tos
Small/Big bandages	Los vendas pequeñas/grandes

Pain-killers	Los analgésicos
Mosquito repellent	El repelente
Medicine	La medicina/El remedio
An inhaler	Un inhalador
An ointment/cream	Una pomade
Antibiotic	Antibiótico
Anti-inflammatory	Anti-inflamatorio

Enfermedades leves (Minor ailments)

I am sick.	Estoy enfermo/a.
I have a cold.	Estoy resfriado/a.
I have a sore throat.	Me duele la garganta.
I have a cough.	Tengo tos.
I have a fever.	Tengo una fiebre.
I've been trembling.	He estado temblando.
I'm dizzy/queasy.	Estoy mareado/a.
I have diarrhea.	Tengo diarrea.
I have a headache.	Tengo dolor de la cabeza.
I'm constipated.	Estoy estreñido/a.
I burned myself.	Me quemé.

Partes del cuerpo (Body parts)

Where does it hurt?	¿Dónde le duele?
It hurts here.	Me duele aquí
My... hurts	Me duele...
Arm	El brazo
Shoulder	El hombre
Hand	La mano
Finger	El dedo
Elbow	El codo
Leg	La pierna
Knee	La rodilla
Foot	El pie
Toes	Los dedos de pie
Back	La espalda
Bottom	El trasero
Head	La cabeza

Eyes	Los ojos
Ears	Las orejas
Nose	La nariz
Mouth	La boca
Teeth	Los dientes

Más frases (More phrases)

I cut myself with a knife.	Me corté con un cuchillo.
I twisted my wrist.	Doblé la muñeca.
I bumped my head.	Me di un golpe en la cabeza.
I sprained my ankle.	Doblé el tobillo.
I fainted.	Me desmayé.
I was throwing up all night.	Estaba vomitando toda la noche.
You should rest and drink lots of liquids.	Ud. debe descansar y tomar muchos líquidos.
You need to take this medicine.	Ud. necesita tomar este medicamento.
Here is your prescription.	Aquí esta la receta.
You should take one pill two times daily.	Debe tomar una píldora doz veces diariamente.
¿Do you have health insurance?	¿Tiene seguro medico?

¡Los Ejercicios!

Match the Vocabulary

1. pain-killers

a. la cabeza

2. An ointment
ojos

b. las gotas para los

3. cough syrup

c. el remedio

4. medicine

d. la pierna

5. eye drops

e. el analgésico

6. arm

f. los ojos

7. leg

g. una pomada

8. head	h. las orejas
9. ears	i. el brazo
10. eyes	j. el jarabe para la tos

Match the Phrases

1. Estoy resfriada.	a. My throat hurts.
2. Tengo una fiebre.	b. I'm constipated.
3. Me duele la garganta.	c. I have a cold.
4. Estoy estreñido.	d. My hand hurts
5. Me duele la mano.	e. I have a fever.

Translate to English

1. Me duele la cabeza.

_____

2. Aquí está la receta.

_____

3. Me corté con un cuchillo.

_____

4. ¿Dónde le duele?

_____

5. He estado temblando.

_____

Illnesses Answers

Match the Vocabulary

1. pain-killers	e. el analgésico
2. an ointment	g. una pomada
3. cough syrup	j. el jarabe para la tos
4. medicine	c. el remedio
5. eye drops	b. las gotas para los ojos
6. arm	i. el brazo

7. leg	d. la pierna
8. head	a. la cabeza
9. ears	h. las orejas
10. eyes	f. los ojos

Match the Phrases

1. Estoy resfriada.	c. I have a cold.
2. Tengo una fiebre.	e. I have a fever.
3. Me duele la garganta.	a. My throat hurts.
4. Estoy estreñido.	b. I'm constipated.
5. Me duele la mano.	d. My hand hurts

Translate to English

1. Me duele la cabeza.	<u>My head hurts.</u>
2. Aquí está la receta.	<u>Here is the prescription.</u>
3. Me corté con un cuchillo.	<u>I cut myself with a knife.</u>
4. ¿Dónde le duele?	<u>Where does it hurt?</u>
5. He estado temblando.	<u>I have been trembling.</u>

Emergencias (Emergencies)

Emergency room	La sala de urgencia
To call for an ambulance	Llamar a una ambulancia
To call for firefighters.	Llamar a los bomberos.
To call the police.	Llamar a la policia.
Emergency phone number	Número de teléfono de emergencia
Help!	¡Socorro!
Fire!	¡Fuego!
Call a doctor/911!	¡Llame a un medico/al número de emergencia!
Can you help me?	¿Me puede ayudar?
Can you take me to the hospital?	¿Me puede llevar al hospital?
May I use your phone?	¿Puedo usar su teléfono?

¡Ojo! The phone number for general emergencies in Spain is 112

Ayúdeme (Help me!)

He/She...	Él/Ella...
is hurt.	está herido/a.
is unconscious.	está inconsciente.
fell down the stairs.	se cayó en la escalera.
is not breathing.	no está respirando.
is bleeding a lot.	está sangrando mucho.
had a heart attack.	tuvo un infarto.
He/she was run over by a car.	Lo/la atropellaron.
I can't feel his/her pulse.	No siento su pulso.

Necesito... (I need...)

To go to the police station.	Ir a la estación de policía.
A lawyer.	Un/a abogado/a.
To file a complaint.	Presentar una queja.
To report a robbery/accident.	Informar un robo/accidente.
To report the loss of my passport.	Informar la pérdida mi pasaporte.
To call the embassy.	Llamar a la embajada.
Money for bail.	Dinero para la fianza.

¿Qué le paso? (What happened to you?)

Someone stole my phone in the subway.	En el metro, alguien me robó el teléfono.
Someone stole my purse on the street.	Alguien me robó la cartera en la calle.
I lost my passport.	Perdí mi pasaporte.
I got in a car accident.	Tuve un accidente del carro.
I got ripped off.	Alguien me engañó.
Someone took my credit card.	Alguien robó mi tarjeta de crédito.
I need to cancel my credit card.	Necesito cancelar mi tarjeta de crédito

¡Los Ejercicios!

Match the Phrases

1. La sala de urgencia------ a. Call a doctor.
2. ¿Puedo usar su teléfono? ------ b. The emergency room
3. Llame a un médico ------ c. Can you help me?
4. ¿Me puede ayudar? ------ d. She is hurt.
5. Ella está herida. ------ e. May I use your phone?

Fill in the blank with the word from the word bank and translate

embajada------ presentar------ robo
fianza------ estación------ Llamar

1. Me gustaría ir a la _____ de policia.

2. Necesito _____ una queja.

3. Quiero llamar a la _____.

4. Necesito dinero para la _____.

5. Quisiera informar un _____.

Translate to Spanish
1. Someone stole my phone in the subway.
   _____

2. She is unconscious
   _____

3. I got ripped off.
   _____

4. He is not breathing.
   _____

5. She is bleeding a lot.
   _____

Emergencies Answers

Match the Phrases

1. La sala de urgencia ------ b. The emergency room
                                  2. ¿Puedo usar su teléfono? -----

- e. May I use your phone?

3. Llame a un médico ------ a. Call a doctor.

4. ¿Me puede ayudar? ------ c. Can you help me?

5. Ella está herida. ------ d. She is hurt.

Fill in the blank with the word from the word bank and translate

1. Me gustaría ir a la <u>estación </u>de policia. ------ <u>I would like to go to the police</u> <u>station.</u>

2. Necesito <u>presentar</u> una queja. ------ <u>I need to report a complaint.</u>

3. Quiero llamar a la <u>embajada.</u> ------ <u>I want to call the embassy.</u>

4. Necesito dinero para la <u>fianza</u>. ------ <u>I need money for bail.</u>

5. Quisiera informar un <u>robo</u>. ------ <u>I need to report a robbery.</u>

Translate to Spanish

1. Someone stole my phone in the subway. ------ <u>Alguien me robó el teléfono en</u> <u>el metro.</u>

2. She is unconscious------ <u>Ella está inconsciente.</u>

3. I got ripped off. ------ <u>Alguien me engañó</u>

4. He is not breathing. ------ <u>Él no está respirando.</u>

5. She is bleeding a lot. ------ <u>Ella está sangrando mucho.</u>

Money in the Bank

Taking care of your finances in a foreign country is another daunting task to deal with. Luckily in most countries you can just use your ATM card in *la cajera automática* (the ATM machine) and receive the country's currency for a small fee. There is a possibility that you will have to go to the bank whether it be to transfer money, exchange money, or open a bank account if you do plan on staying for a longer period of time. Here are some phrases to help in case you do need to make a trip to the bank.

Banking Phrases

I need to wire money internationally.	Necesito mandar dinero internacionalmente.
I would like to withdraw cash.	Quisiera retirar dinero.
Currency	Moneda

May I cash my traveler's checks?	¿Puedo cobrar mis cheques viajeros?
Deposit money	Depositar dinero
Exchange money	Cambiar dinero
How much is the dollar worth?	¿A cómo está el dólar?
I want to open an account.	Quiero abrir una cuenta.
I want to transfer money.	Quiero transferir dinero.
Cash	En efectivo

In Spain, they use the Euro as their currency. The current rate is 1 EUR = $1.24 USD

Hay un problema... (There is a problem...)

You don't have enough money in your account.	No hay suficiente dinero en su cuenta.
My card has been swallowed by the ATM.	El cajero automático ha tragado mi tarjeta.
I can't withdraw any cash.	No puedo sacar dinero.
There is an error message on the machine.	Hay un mensaje de error en la máquina.
I don't know how to withdraw money.	No sé sacar dinero.
I can't select credit card.	No puedo seleccionar tarjeta de crédito.

Más vocabulario – En el banco

(More vocabulary- In the bank)

Debit card	Tarjeta de débito
Credit card	Tarjeta de crédito
To transfer	Transferir
Account	La cuenta
Cashier	El cajero
To take out a loan	Sacar un préstamo
Identification (ID)	La identificación (ID)
Amount	La cantidad

¡Los Ejercicios!

Fill in the blank with the word from the word bank

una cuenta ------ cheques viajeros ------ dinero
mandar------ un préstamo------ moneda

1. Quisiera sacar _____.
2. ¿Puedo cobrar mis _____?
3. Quisiera abrir _____.
4. Necesito _____ dinero internacionalmente.
5. No hay suficiente _____ en su cuenta.

Translate to English

1. No sé sacar dinero.

_____

2. Quiero transferir dinero.

_____

3. ¿A cómo está el dólar?

_____

4. El cajero automático ha tragado mi tarjeta.

_____

5. Hay un mensaje de error en la máquina

_____

Money in the Bank Answers

Fill in the blank with the word from the word bank

1. Quisiera sacar un préstamo.
2. ¿Puedo cobrar mis cheques viajeros?
3. Quisiera abrir una cuenta.
4. Necesito mandar dinero internacionalmente.
5. No hay suficiente dinero en su cuenta.

Translate to English

1. No sé sacar dinero.   I don't know how to withdraw money.

2. Quiero transferir dinero.   I want to transfer money.

3. ¿A cómo está el dólar?   How much is the dollar worth?

4. El cajero automático ha tragado mi tarjeta. The ATM has swallowed my card.

5. Hay un mensaje de error en la máquina   There is an error message on the machine.

Time will tell

As I mentioned in the introduction, Spanish-speakers often have a very different concept of time. Expect people to arrive at least 2 hours late to social events. When it comes to work and school matters, the people tend to be more punctual. However, I can remember showing up to classes on time when I studied abroad in Chile and sometimes being the only one there, sitting alone in a medium sized auditorium looking around at the empty chairs. In about 15 to 30 minutes the other students and professor would come shuffling into class. You should still show up on time though just in case you have one of the punctual professors. In this section, we will discuss how to ask and say what time it is, the days of the week and the date.

¿Qué hora es? (What time is it?)

It's one.	Es la una. (You only use 'es la' for times with 1)
It's two.	Son las dos... (*Son las* is used for times 2-12)
It's seven thirty.	Son las siete y media. (Or 'Son las siete y treinta)
It's fifteen 'til ten.	Son las diez menos quince.
It's a quarter 'til five.	Son las cinco menos cuarto.
It's five 'til three.	Son las tres menos cinco. (You switch the numbers, 'five 'til three' turns into 'three minus five')
a.m. (in the morning)	de la mañana
p.m. (in the afternoon)	de la tarde
p.m. (at night)	de la noche

¡Ojo! If you need to add minutes to your time, just add the word '*y*'

For example: It is 3:10 = Son las tres y diez

¿Qué día es hoy? (What day is Today?)

Today is Tuesday.	Hoy es martes.
Today	Hoy
Yesterday	Ayer
Tomorrow	Mañana
The day after tomorrow.	Pasado mañana.
The day before yesterday.	Anteayer.
Monday	el lunes
Tuesday	el martes
Wednesday	el miércoles
Thursday	el jueves
Friday	el Viernes
Saturday	el sábado
Sunday	el domingo

¡Ojo! When you need to say that something is happening on a particular day of the week, you say, *'El lunes, tengo la práctica de beisbol'* = 'On Monday, I have baseball practice. You DON'T need to say 'on'.

¿Cuál es la fecha hoy? (What is the date today?)

Today is May 20th.	Hoy es el veinte de mayo.
It is June 1st.	Es el primero de junio.
January	enero
February	febrero
March	marzo
April	abril
May	mayo
June	junio
July	julio
August	agosto
September	septiembre
October	octubre
November	noviembre

December	diciembre

In order to say the date in Spanish

el + (número) + de + (mes)

the + (number) + of + (month

¡Los Ejercicios!

Find the correct sentence for each group and translate.

1.
___ Son la una de la tarde.
___ Es la una de la tarde.
___ Es las una de la tarde.

_____

2.
___ Es el veintisiete de abril.
___ Es la veintisiete de abril.
___ Es el abril de veintisiete.

_____

3.
___ Es las cinco de la mañana.
___ Son la cinco de la mañana.
___ Son las cinco de la mañana.

_____

4.
___ Son las siete menos cuarto.
___ Son las cuarto menos siete.
___ Son menos siete las cuarto

_____

Unscramble and translate the months

1. oarmz   _____

112

2. ebevoimrn _____

3. oeern _____

4. oijnu _____

5. tebcuro _____

6. oeerrbf _____

7. lbair _____

8. oijlu _____

9. ymoa _____

10. eeebpsitmr _____

Translate to Spanish

1. Today is Wednesday.

_____

2. It is December 25th.

_____

3. It is fifteen 'til five.

_____

4. Tomorrow is Friday.

_____

5. It is 9:00 at night.

_____

Time will tell Answers

Find the correct sentence for each group and translate.

1.
___ Son la una de la tarde.
x_ Es la una de la tarde.
___ Es las una de la tarde.   It's one in the afternoon.

2.

x   Es el veintisiete de abril.

___ Es la veintisiete de abril.

___ Es el abril de veintisiete.   It's April 27th.

3.

___ Es las cinco de la mañana.

___ Son la cinco de la mañana.

x   Son las cinco de la mañana.   It's five in the morning.

4.

x Son las siete menos cuarto.

___ Son las cuarto menos siete.

___ Son menos siete las cuarto   It's a quarter 'til seven.

Unscramble and translate the months

1. oarmz   marzo - March
2. ebevoimrn   noviembre - November

3. oeern   enero - January

4. oijnu   junio - June
5. tebcuro   octubre - October
6. oeerrbf   febrero - February

7. lbair   abril – April

8. oijlu   julio - July

9. ymoa   mayo - May
10. eeebpsitmr   septiembre - September

Translate to Spanish

1. Today is Wednesday.   Hoy es miércoles.
2. It is December 25th.   Es el veinticinco de diciembre.
3. It is fifteen 'til five.   Son las cinco menos quince.
4. Tomorrow is Friday.   Mañana es viernes.
5. It is 9:00 at night.   Son las nueve de la noche.

How's the Weather?

Knowing how to communicate about the weather is another important topic to know. Especially in those tropical Spanish-speaking countries in which it will be sunny and hot one second and pouring rain with hurricane like wind, the next. You need to be able to know when to snatch that **paraguas** (umbrella) or **permeable** (raincoat) on your way out the door. Though in some countries I would recommend it no matter what due to the unpredictability of the weather. Be sure to watch out for the hurricanes that occur often in the Carribean, Mexico, and Central America. Also, try to get used to sweating the small stuff because in most Spanish-speaking countries central air-conditioning is not common and you are more likely to be walking than driving around. Also don't forget your **bloqueador** (sunscreen). In Latin American countries the sun is typically much stronger than what we are used to. Here are some words and phrases to help you understand and talk about the weather.

¿Qué tiempo hace hoy? (What is the weather like today)

What's the weather like today?	¿Cómo está el tiempo hoy?
It is cold	Hace frío
It is hot	Hace calor
It is sunny	Hace sol
It is windy	Hace viento
It is very cold, hot, etc.	Hace mucho frío, calor, etc.(Notice with these phrases you use 'mucho' not 'muy' to say 'very'.
The weather is nice	Hace buen tiempo
The weather is bad	Hace mal tiempo
It's cool.	Hace fresco
It's raining.	Está lloviendo
Is it going to rain today?	¿Va a llover hoy?
Yes, it's going to rain, No, it's not going to rain	Sí va a llover/No, no va a llover
It's snowing	Está nevando
It's foggy.	Hay niebla.
It's misty.	Hay neblina.
It's lightning.	Hay relámpagos.

It's humid.	Está húmedo.
It's just sprinkling.	Sólo está lloviznando.
It's raining hard.	Está lloviendo mucho.
It's hailing.	Hay granizos.
It's thundering outside.	Está tronando afuera.
The sun is coming up.	Está amaneciendo el sol.
The sun is goind down.	Está atardeciendo el sol.
It's dark.	Está oscuro.
Really?	¿De veras?
Sunscreen	El bloqueador
Raincoat	El permeable
Umbrella	El paraguas or La sombrilla.

¡Los Ejercicios!

Match the Phrases

1. Está nevando.
2. ¿Hace calor?
3. Hace frío.
4. Está lloviendo.
rain.
5. No va a llover.

a. It's raining
b. It's cold.
c. Is it hot?
d. It's not going to

e. It's snowing.

Translate to Spanish

1. Is it going to rain today?

   _____

2. It's thundering outside

   _____

3. It's raining hard.

   _____

4. The weather is nice today.

   _____

5. It's very hot today.

   _____

How's the Weather? Answers

Match the Phrases

1. Está nevando. ------ e. It's snowing.
2. ¿Hace calor? ------ c. Is it hot?
3. Hace frío. ------ b. It's cold.
4. Está lloviendo. ------ a. It's raining
5. No va a llover. ------ d. It's not going to rain.

Translate to Spanish

1. Is it going to rain today? ------ ¿Va a llover hoy?
2. It's thundering outside------ Está tronando afuera.
3. It's raining hard. ------ Está lloviendo mucho
4. The weather is nice today. ------ Hace buen tiempo hoy.
5. It's very hot today. ------ Hace mucho calor hoy.

Chapter 6
Extra Material You'll Definitely Use Down the Road

This chapter includes some extra topics that you will find useful including going to the supermarket, maintaining your health and beauty, and dealing with computers and internet.

-The Supermarket

- Pamper yourself!

-WorldWideWeb

The Supermarket

This section will help you you to go grocery shopping in Spanish. We all know what it is like to be in a new supermarket and have no idea where anything is. Especially in a new country. You of course will notice a few things that are different from our supermarkets. First of all, you usually have to put your bag in a locker. You are not allowed to carry bags into the supermarket to prevent shoplifting incidences. Another thing to be prepared for is that you must weigh your produce at the stand instead of the cashier doing it for you when you pay. Either you or an employee will weigh and it will print a little sticker to put on your produce. I also added the phrase ***¿Tienes cambio?*** *(*Do you have change) to help you since the cashiers are almost always short on change. I have found this to be true in almost any foreign country I have visited. So make sure to have change with you on those grocery shopping trips. These phrases will help you to survive the Spanish supermarket.

El Supermercado (Supermarket)

Where is/are ...?	¿Dónde está/están...?
Fruits and vegetables.	las frutas y verduras.
Dairy products	los productos lácteos
Fish	el pescado.
Meat and deli section	la sección de la carnicería.
Bread	el pan.
Drinks	las bebidas.
Pharmacy and Beauty	la área de farmacía y belleza.

Frozen items	los artículos congelados.

Busco... (I am looking for...)

A toothbrush	Un cepillo de dientes.
Toothpaste	Una pasta de dientes.
Coffee and tea	Café y té
The toiletpaper	El papel de baño
The cracker and cookies aisle	El pasillo de galletas.
The paper goods.	Los artículos de papel.
The sauces and dressings.	Las salsas y aderezos.
The bakery and pastry section.	La sección de la panadería y pastelería.

¡Los Ejercicios!

Match the Phrases

1. Busco un cepillo de dientes. ------ a. Where are the drinks?
2. ¿Dónde está el pescado? ------ b. I am looking for sauces and dressings.
3. Busco las salsas y aderezos. ------ c. I would like the bakery and pastry section.
4. ¿Dónde están las bebidas? ------ d. Where is the fish?
5. Quisiera la sección de la panadería y pastelería ------ e. I am looking for a toothbrush.

Translate to English

1. ¿Dónde está la sección de la carnicería?

_____

2. Busco el café y té.

_____

3. ¿Dónde está el pan?

_____

4. Busco el pasillo de galletas.

_____

5. ¿Dónde están los artículos congelados?

_____

The Supermarket Answers

Match the Phrases

1. Busco un cepillo de dientes. ------ e. I am looking for a toothbrush.
2. ¿Dónde está el pescado? ------ d. Where is the fish?
3. Busco las salsas y aderezos. ------ b. I am looking for sauces and dressings
4. ¿Dónde están las bebidas? ------ a. Where are the drinks?
5. Quisiera la sección de la panadería y pastelería. ------ c. I would like the bakery and pastry section

Translate to English

1. ¿Dónde está la sección de la carnicería?   Where is the deli section?
2. Busco el café y té.   I'm looking for the coffee and tea.
3. ¿Dónde está el pan?   Where is the bread?
4. Busco el pasillo de galletas.   I am looking for the cracker aisle.
5. ¿Dónde están los artículos congelados?   Where are the frozen ítems?

Pamper yourself!

Travelling and learning a foreign language can be sooooo stressful. This chapter will help you to pamper yourself and look good by going to that spa, beauty salon, nail salon, or whatever your preferred place of pampering is. Remember to breathe in, out, and relax!

La Salud y la Belleza (Health and Beauty)

I would like to get…	Quisiera hacerme…
A facial.	Un facial.
A manicure.	Una manicura.
A pedicure.	Una pedicura.
A wax.	Una depilación con cera
A massage.	Un masaje.
An exfoliation.	Una exfoliación.
I would like get my hair and make-up done.	Quisiera arreglarme el pelo y maquillarme.

Artículos de Belleza (Beauty Items)

What would you like to buy?	¿Qué quisiera comprar?
I would like to buy...	Quisiera comprar...
A nail polish.	Esmalte para las uñas.
A nail polish remover.	Quitaesmalte
A nail file.	Una lema de uñas.
A nail clipper.	Un cortador de uñas.
A perfume.	Un perfume.
Tweezers.	Pinzas.
Hair dye.	Tinta para el cabello.
A moisturizer	Una loción hidratante.
An anti-wrinkle cream.	Una crema anti-arrugas.
Make-up	Maquillaje.
A make-up remover.	Un desmaqillador.
An eyeliner.	Un lápiz de ojos.
A mascara.	Una mascara, pestañita.
An eye shadow.	Una sombra de ojos.
A lip gloss.	Un brillo de labios.
A lipstick.	Un lápiz de labios.
A brush (for cheeks)	Una brocha.
A brush (for eyeliner/nail polish)	Un píncel.
A concealer.	Un corrector.
A foundation.	Un base.
A blush.	Un rubor.

¡Los Ejercicios!

Choose the correct answer from the parentheses and translate.
1. Quisiera _____ el pelo (arreglarme/manicura).

_____

2. Quiero _____ (una lema de uñas /una lema con uñas).

_____

3. Quisiera comprar _____ (unas pinzas/unos pinzas).

_____

4. Quisiera hacerme _____ (Un masaje/Una masage).

_____

5. Me gustaría comprar _____ (Maquillaje/Maquillarme).

_____

Match the Vocabulary

1. Remueve esmalte	a. a brush
2. Un desmaquillador	b. an anti-wrinkle cream
3. Un corrector	c. a foundation
4. Un base	d. a lipgloss
5. Un brillo de labios remover	e. a nail polish
6. Una sombre de ojos	f. a concealer
7. Un lápiz de labios remover	g. a make-up
8. Una crema anti-arrugas	h. a nail clipper
9. Un píncel	i. an eyeshadow
10. Un cortador de uñas	j. a lipstick

Peluquería (Hair salon)

Shampoo	Champú
Haircut	Corte de pelo.
Coloring	Tintar
Highlights	Mechas
Perm	Permanente
Conditioning treatment	Tratamientos hidratantes.
Blow-dry	Secar el pelo.
Chemical Straightening.	Alisado químico
Straightening (With flat iron)	Planchado.
Curlers.	Rolos.

Cortes de pelo (Haircuts)

What haircut would you like?	¿Cuál corte le gustaría hacer?
Like in this picture.	Así como esta foto.
Layered	Con capas.
Assymetrical haircut.	Corte Asimétrico.
Layered on top.	Con capas encima.
Short and layered.	Corto y con capas.

Bangs.	Los flequillos.
A trim.	Sólo cortar los puntitos.

Cuidado, tengo... (Careful, I have...)

Dry skin	La piel seca
Oily skin	La piel grasosa
Combination skin	La piel seca y grasosa
Sensitive skin	La piel sensible
Dark complexión	La piel morena
Fair complexión	La piel blanca
Fine hair	El cabello muy fino
Thick hair	El cabello muy grueso
Greasy hair	El cabello grasoso
Dry hair	El cabello seco
Curly hair	El cabello rizado
Frizzy hair	El cabello crespo
Damaged hair	El cabello dañado
Dyed hair	El cabello tintado
Permed hair	El cabello con permanente
Wavy hair	El cabello ondulado
Dandruff	La caspa

Translate to English

1. Quisiera un corte de pelo.

   _____

2. ¿Cuál corte le gustaría hacer?

   _____

3. Me gustaría corto y con capas.

   _____

4. Cuidado, tengo el cabello dañado.

   _____

5. Me gustaría un corte con flequillos.

   _____

Pamper Yourself! Answers

Choose the correct answer from the parentheses and translate.

1. Quisiera <u>arreglarme</u> el pelo (arreglarme/manicura).

<u>I would like to get my hair fixed.</u>

2. Quiero <u>una lema de uñas</u> (una lema de uñas /una lema con uñas).

<u>I want a nail file.</u>

3. Quisiera comprar <u>unas pinzas</u> (unas pinzas/unos pinzas).

<u>I would like to buy some tweezers.</u>

4. Quisiera hacerme <u>un masaje</u> (Un masaje/Una masage).

<u>I would like to get a massage.</u>

5. Me gustaría comprar <u>maquillaje</u> (Maquillaje/Maquillarme).

<u>I would like to buy make-up.</u>

Match the Vocabulary

1. Remueve esmalte------e. a nail polish remover
2. Un desmaquillador------ g. a make-up remover
3. Un corrector------ f. a concealer
4. Un base ------ c. a foundation
5. Un brillo de labios------ d. a lipgloss
6. Una sombre de ojos------ i. an eyeshadow
7. Un lápiz de labios------ j. a lipstick
8. Una crema anti-arrugas------ b. an anti-wrinkle cream
9. Un píncel------ a. a brush
10. Un cortador de uñas ------ h. nail clippers

Translate to English
1. Quisiera un corte de pelo. ------ <u>I would like a haircut.</u>
2. ¿Cuál corte le gustaría hacer? ------ <u>Which cut would you like to do?</u>
3. Me gustaría corto y con capas.. ------ <u>I would like it short with layers.</u>
4. Cuidado, tengo el cabello dañado. ------ <u>Careful, I have damaged hair.</u>
5. Me gustaría un corte con flequillos. ------ <u>I would like a cut with bangs.</u>

This last section will help you with any dealings you have with the internet or computers. It could be having to go to a **cyber café** (Internet café) or trying to get your internet installed. Luckily much of the vocabulary that has to do with Internet and technology has been adopted from English to Spanish making the words much easier. One tip is to put your computer or phone in Spanish before your trip. That way you can start to learn the vocabulary in context. With the ever growing importance and presence of the Internet in our lives, these vocabulary words and phrases will be essential and surely frequently used on your trip. This section will complete the academic part of the book to help prepare you for your travels to a Spanish speaking country. We will next delve into where to travel in Spain, Spanish slang and the best language-learning websites. Here are some vocabulary words and phrases to help you discuss the Internet.

Vocabulario del Computador (Computer Vocabulary)

Computer	El computador
Laptop	El notebook or Computador Móvil
Mouse	El ratón or El mouse
Keyboard	El teclador
Screen	La pantalla
Software	El software
Driver	El driver
Hardware	El hardware

¡Ojo! Notice that many words that have to do with technology are said the same way in both languages. In Spanish, you will just have to say the word according to the Spanish pronunciation.

Por favor, me ayuda, necesito... (Please, help me, I need...)

To turn on the computer.	Encender el computador.
To turn off the computer.	Apagar el computador.
To reboot the computer.	Reinicar el computador.
To turn on the screen.	Encender la pantalla.
To click here.	Hacer clic aquí.

To delete.	Eliminar.
To press enter.	Presionar enter.
To press escape.	Presionar escape.
To log in.	Iniciar sesión.
To log out.	Cerrar session
To save.	Guardar.
To print something.	Imprimir algo.

Navegando por el Internet

(Finding your way around the Internet)

Headphones	Audífonos
Microphone	Mícrofono
Webcam	Cámara web
Email (formal)	Correo electrónico
Email (informal)	Email
Browser	Navegador
Website	Sitio web
Homepage	Página inicial
Webpage	Página web
Chatroom	Sala de chat

Ayúdame, necesito... (Help me, I need to...)

To go online.	Conectarme
To surf (the web).	Navegar la red
To check my emails.	Revisar mi email.
To send an email.	Mandar un email.
To attach a document.	Adjuntar un documento.
To download the attachment.	Bajar un documento.
To scroll up/down.	Desplazarlo hacia arriba/abajo
To open a new document.	Abrir un documento nuevo
To use Skype.	Usar skype.

¡Los Ejercicios!

Match the Vocabulary

1. La pantalla ------ a. Email
2. El ratón ------ b. Homepage
3. El teclador------ c. To send
4. Audífonos ------ d. To print
5. Micrófono------ e. To attach
6. Correo electrónico ------ f. The mouse
7. Página inicial------ g. Headphones
8. Imprimir------ h. Microphone
9. Adjuntar------ i. The screen
10. Mandar------ j. The keyboard

Match the Phrases

1. Necesito conectarme.   a. I want to save this document
2. Quisiera reinicar el computador.   b. I would like to print something.
3. Quiero guardar este documento.   c. I need to get online.
4. Necesitas cerrar la sesión.   d. I would like to restart the computer.
5. Me gustaría imprimir algo.   e. You need to logout.

Translate to English

1. Quisiera encender el computador.

   _____

2. ¿Necesitas encender la pantalla?

   _____

3. Necesito abrir un navegador.

   _____

4. ¿Te gustaría desplazarlo hacia abajo?

   _____

5. Me gustaría bajar un documento.

   _____

World Wide Web Answers

Match the Vocabulary

1. La pantalla   i. The screen

2. El ratón   f. The mouse
3. El teclador   j. The keyboard

4. Audífonos   g. Headphones

5. Micrófono   h. Microphone

6. Correo electrónico a. Email

7. Página inicial   b. Homepage

8. Imprimir   d. To print
9. Adjuntar   e. To attach

10. Mandar   c. To send

Match the Phrases

1. Necesito conectarme.   c. I need to get online.
2. Quisiera reinicar el computador.   d. I would like to restart the computer.

3. Quiero guardar este documento.   a. I want to save this document

4. Necesitas cerrar la sesión.   e. You need to logout.
5. Me gustaría imprimir algo.   b. I would like to print something.

Translate to English

1. Quisiera encender el computador.

I would like to turn on the computer.

2. ¿Necesitas encender la pantalla?

Do you need to turn on the screen?

3. Necesito abrir un navegador.

I need to open a browser.

4. ¿Te gustaría desplazarlo hacia abajo?

Would you like to scroll down?

5. Me gustaría bajar un documento.

I would like to download a document.

Chapter 7
The Top Ten, Most Beautiful Places to Visit In Spain

This section will give you advice on Spain's top ten must-see destinations along with listing some common slang used in Spain. It includes the location and description of some renowned and colorful festivals of Spain. The Spanish can find almost any reason to celebrate, from throwing tomatoes to the most famous and precarious of getting chased by bulls. Along with this, we will include some of the best websites for learning the Spanish language. Some websites are picked due to their detailed explanations and others because of the variety of games that they provide to practice the language. Enjoy travelling Spain and the web in this chapter!

Top ten places to visit in Spain

1. Barcelona

Barcelona is probably the favorite Spanish city for most travelers. It is not the capital but it is admired due to its beautiful artchitecture, five kilometers of beach, and the best football (soccer) team in the world. It contains some of the best modernist buildings in the world. The city's positive energy and creative cuisine make it a destination must while in Spain.

2. Madrid

The capital of Spain may not be as classically beautiful as Barcelona, but it has some of the world's best museums. These include the Prado, the Reina Sofia, and the Thyssen-Bornemisza. Along with this, Madrid is filled with beautiful parks, shopping variety, and outstanding nightlife. Whether you are enjoying the famous breakfast of Madrid of chocolate and churros, going to *La Latina Barrio* to *tapear* (Going from bar to bar ordering drinks and free tapas) or escaping for some peace and quiet to *El Retiro,* a park in the middle of the city, Madrid has plenty for a world wanderer to enjoy.

3. Seville

Seville is the home to many of the trademarks that Spain is known for. First, it is the birthplace of *el* flamenco the dramatic music and dance of *los gitanos* (gypsies). Secondly, it is one of the most famous cities in Spain for the world renowned Spanish bullfighting. Seville is also known for its Moorish architecture and contains Europe's largest cathedral along with the Alcázar de Seville, a breath-taking royal palace that was once a Moorish fort dating back to the 1300's.

4. Valencia

Valencia is Spain's third largest city and largely known for its street life. Due to its pleasant climate, the streetlife is active during the day and night. It is also known for its world-famous architecture of the home-grown architect Santiago Calatreva. Along with this, Valencia's golden sandy beaches provide for breath-taking views of the Mediterranean. It is also home to the delicious paella, sometimes considered Spain's national dish.

5.Bilbao

Bilbao is known for its iconic building, the Guggenheim. It is a pleasant port city surrounded by hills with plenty of alleyways to explore and try out the thriving Basque cuisine. It has a variety of museums and galleries worth visiting and a beautiful surrounding countryside that allows for many outdoor activities.

6. Granada

 Granada has been a cultural center in Europe since the 1200's. It is home to Spain's most visited monument, the Alhambra, which is both a palace and a fortress surrounded by walls, along with other buildings from the same era.

7. Cordoba

Cordoba is located in Andalusia, in Southern Spain. Most of the attractions are situated in what used to be its Jewish and Moorish quarters. They are filled with narrow cobbed streets in which you can find one of the best mosques in the world, the Great Mosque along with a royal palace fortress.

8. Toledo

Toledo was once a melting pot of Jewish, Muslim, and Christian cultures which makes for an interesting combination of architecture in the city. The city, built on a hill fairly close to Madrid, has a diverse assortment of monuments. Toledo was once home to the outstanding artist, El Greco, and as a result exhibits many of his masterpieces. The one monument you must visit is Toledo's extravagant cathedral, one of the largest in the world.

9. Salamanca

Salamanca is a city located in Northwestern Spain. It is most well known for being home to one of Europe's oldest universities that is spread throughout the city center. In Salamanca, you can enjoy some of the greatest architecture of Spain, one of the most splendid squares of Europe, two magnificent cathedrals, and the many glowing golden stone buildings found throughout the city.

10. Santiago de Compostela

Santiago de Compostela, the capital of Galicia also in Northwestern Spain, though, not a very large city, is known as a very popular pilgrimage destination for Christians. It exhibits a mixture of Romanesque, Gothic, and Baroque arquitecture. In this city you can appreciate a towering landmark cathedral, the Plaza de Obradoiro, and Convent San Martiño Pinario, a baroque Convent.

Bonus City!
Bunol

Bunol is included as a bonus because it is home to the very peculiar festival called *La Tomatina.* This exciting and messy festival's main feature is a huge tomato fight. The rules of the festival include squishing the tomato before throwing, wearing protective safety goggles and gloves, and not bringing any glass items or items that if thrown could do harm. Water cannons signal the start and finish of this food fight, which takes place on the last Wednesday of August. The festival actually lasts for a week and includes, parades, music, dancing, fireworks, and culminates with the tomato food fight.

Common slang used in Spain

This section will help you to learn to speak like a native.

Spanish Slang	English Meaning
Apuntarse (¡Me apunto! I agree!)	To accompany others or do what others do

Boli	Pen
Caer gordo (Me cae gordo este professor. I don't agree with this teacher)	To not agree with something or someone
Colado/Colao	Someone who enters to places uninvited and without paying
Estar colado por alguien.	To be very much in love.
Cotillear	To gossip or be nosy.
Dar la lata	To bug, annoy, bother
De cajón	Obvious
Echarme una siesta	Take a nap/Lie down for a nap
Gazpacho	A mess or dilemma
¡Es la caña!	It's awesome!
Está en el quinto pino.	It's very far away/out in the boondocks.
¡Está como un cencerro!	He/she/it is crazy.
Gente maja	Pleasant and generous person
Hincha	Fan of a particular soccer team
Mala pata	Bad luck
La marcha	Nightlife (Refers to the energy of the night life in Spain, the whole going out process of dancing, eating, drinking, and socializing.)
Matar	To annoy
Me importa un pimiento.	I don't care.
¡Me lo pasé pipa!	I had a great time!
Movida	A party
Móvil	Cell phone
Ni fu ni fa	It doesn't matter to me. (expresses indifference)
¡Olé!	Yay!
Pasta	Money
Pijo	An insult to a rich kid with poor taste.
¡Qué chulo/a!	Cool!
¡Qué fuerte!	No way!/I can't believe it!
¡Qué guay!	Cool!
Tapear	To eat tapas; to go from bar to bar eating tapas
Tapeo	The noun of tapear; refers to the act of going to bars and eating tapas

Tertulia	Occurs when people meet together to have small talk; chit chat.
Tía	A chick; literally means aunt
Tía Buena	A beautiful woman; literally means good aunt
Tío	A guy; dude
Vale	Ok; sure; I agree
¡Venga, hombre!	Yeah, right!; You have to be kidding!
¡Véte a freir espárragos!	Go away/Go take a hike/Leave me alone
Viejo verde	Dirty old man

Great language-learning websites

To finish the book, I will recommend some great websites you can use to practice Spanish. Some include more than one languages in case you want to tackle another language along with Spanish. They provide you with games to practice vocabulary use and grammar, audio support, and verb conjugation practice. Something most of the websites have in common is they use repetition of the vocabulary in different ways to help you memorize it, a great language tool! I tried to cut it down to ten, and then to fifteen but there were so many good ones, my final cut included sixteen web sites. I had so much fun going through the websites and trying them out. I even tried some of them out in languages I know nothing about to see what it is like for a beginning learner.

1. BBC Languages Mi vida Loca – This website has a different way of teaching you Spanish. It contains an interactive drama for beginners in Spanish. It takes you on a mystery adventure through Madrid and includes the major grammar points for beginning learners of Spanish. Each episode is accompanied by a learning section with its vocabulary and grammar.

http://www.bbc.co.uk/languages/spanish/mividaloca/

2. Busuu – You have to join and create a login to this page. It is divided into lessons for beginners. It presents the vocabulary to you then tests you on it. It is nice because you are able to set learning goals and track your progress.

http://www.busuu.com/learn-spanish-online

3. Vocabulix – This site gives you the option of creating a login or skipping it to learn without registration. It is divided into five sections, vocabulary (multiple choice), vocabulary (spelling), verbs, grammar, and reading. With this one, you can also track your progress.

http://www.vocabulix.com/

4. Duolingo – This site is very user friendly with great graphics. You can set daily goals and if you create a profile, save your progress. You have a choice of starting with beginning Spanish or taking a placement test. Overall, it has the best graphics out of these websites.

https://www.duolingo.com/

5. Memrise – This site has courses on multiple subjects. You can learn several languages throuth this interactive learning site. It contains 300 words and phrases in Spanish. You have an option of upgrading for a pay membership.

http://www.memrise.com/home/

6. Live Mocha – This site is different because you exchange learning a language from native speakers for teaching one. For example, you are able to play games to learn Spanish in exchange for teaching another member English. It's great because often understanding our own language more helps us to learn other languages.

http://livemocha.com/

7. Rocket Languages – On this site, you receive a six day free trial. You can then decide if you like their audio, story-based teaching style and upgrade.

http://www.rocketlanguages.com/

8. Conjuguemos – This site is a fun way to practice conjugating all types of verbs in Spanish. It categorizes the different kinds of verbs in Spanish, (stem-changing, irregular, etc.) and provides practice for you in all of the tenses. Along with verb conjugation practice, it has vocabulary and grammar practice.

https://conjuguemos.com/

9. **Quia.com** – Includes a variety of games to help you practice. It features concentration, matching, and flashcard games among others. It includes numerous grammar and vocabulary topics of Spanish.

http://www.quia.com/shared/spanish/

10. **Nulu.com** – With this site, you learn Spanish by having the daily newspaper read to you. You are even able to pick which new's topics are most interesting to you. Sports, technology, business, politics, etc. It is excellent because you not only learn a language, but also learn about Spanish-speaking culture and current events.

https://www.nulu.com/en-us/home

11. **Qlipo** – This site uses a very different and effective approach to language learning. It helps English-speakers learn Spanish through music videos. When you are at the home page, click on 'all songs.' Then you can choose which song to start with. It shows you the video and highlights the lyrics as they are said along with the English translation. You then can review the vocabulary and test yourself on it. It makes language learning even more fun.

http://www.qlipo.com/

12. **Mindsnacks.com** – This site makes mobile apps to learn languages. There are nine very interactive apps intended to help you learn the essentials of basic Spanish.

http://mindsnacks.com/

13. **Spanish Dict**- Not only is this site a dictionary where you can look up single words or phrases from Spanish to English and vice versa, it also has free lessons to help you learn Spanish. Most lessons are in video format from 8 to 20 minutes long. They then provide you with quizzes to test what you have learned. It also provides you with a microphone so your speaking can be checked as well. This site is also great if you need to look up the conjugation of a verb.

http://www.spanishdict.com/

14. Spanish Word a Day- This site does more than just provide a Spanish word a day. It also includes conversation classes, a verb and vocabulary trainer, and several Spanish jokes, sayings, and riddles.

http://www.spanish-word-a-day.com/

15. Instreamia- This is a great site that teaches you the language deductively. You start out listening to sentences in Spanish and you have no idea what they are saying. They have you fill in the blank of what you have heard. They later repeat the same phrases and show you what they mean in English. The site also uses popular music to teach you.

http://www.instreamia.com/class/

16. Digital Dialects- This site has good graphics and is very user friendly. It has several categories with games to practice vocabulary for a beginning to intermediate learner of Spanish. It does have a few vocabulary builders for intermediate to advanced learners and some practice for verb conjugation.

http://www.digitaldialects.com/Spanish.htm

Conclusion
Are You Ready? Your Journey Begins Now!

I hope the phrases and grammar tips in this book will help you to get around and enjoy the Spanish-speaking country or countries of your choice. Remember to keep an open mind and be willing to make mistakes when you are trying out a new language. The most important thing is communication. Making a small grammatical error does not always hinder communication. If you have most of the vocabulary correct you still will be able to communicate. And communication is what it is all about. Use the mistakes to learn from and improve your language. Along with this use hints to aid you in communication. These hints could be context clues, gestures, facial expressions, or any other visual cues that can help you understand and communicate with others. Listen to music, play games on your phone, watch movies and TV, and anything else you can think of in Spanish to surround yourself with the language. Use repetition of vocabulary in different ways in your mind to help memorize and retain it. Finally, make use of the great language learning websites I mentioned! This will prepare you even more to travel and communicate in Spain or Latin America. Going abroad and learning a new language can be challenging and occasionally frustrating.

Just remember to stay positive, laugh at yourself and have fun in your travels! Buena suerte y Buen viaje ☺

To your success,

Dagny Taggart

>> Get The Full Spanish Online Course With Audio Lessons <<

If you truly want to learn Spanish 300% FASTER, then hear this out.

I've partnered with the most revolutionary language teachers to bring you the very best Spanish online course I've ever seen. It's a mind-blowing program specifically created for language hackers such as ourselves. It will allow you learn Spanish 3x faster, straight from the comfort of your own home, office, or wherever you may be. It's like having an unfair advantage!

The Online Course consists of:

+ 185 Built-In Lessons
+ 98 Interactive Audio Lessons
+ 24/7 Support to Keep You Going

The program is extremely engaging, fun, and easy-going. You won't even notice you are learning a complex foreign language from scratch. And before you realize it, by the time you go through all the lessons you will officially become a truly solid Spanish speaker.

Old classrooms are a thing of the past. It's time for a language revolution.

If you'd like to go the extra mile, follow the link below and let the revolution begin

>> http://www.bitly.com/Spanish-Course <<

CHECK OUT THE COURSE »

Preview Of "Learn Spanish In 7 DAYS! - The Ultimate Crash Course To Learn The Basics of the Spanish Language In No Time"

Are You ready? It's Time To Learn Spanish!

Most people are daunted by the idea of learning a language. They think it's impossible, even unfathomable. I remember as a junior in high school, watching footage of Jackie O giving a speech in French. I was so impressed and inspired by the ease at which she spoke this other language of which I could not understand one single word.

At that moment, I knew I had to learn at least one foreign language. I started with Spanish, later took on Mandarin, and most recently have started learning Portuguese. No matter how challenging and unattainable it may seem, millions of people have done it. You do NOT have to be a genius to learn another language. You DO have to be willing to take risks and make mistakes, sometimes even make a fool of yourself, be dedicated, and of course, practice, practice, practice!

This book will only provide you with the basics in order to get started learning the Spanish language. It is geared towards those who are planning to travel to a Spanish-speaking country and covers many common scenarios you may find yourself in so feel free to skip around to the topic that is most prudent to you at the moment. It is also focused on the Spanish of Latin America rather than Spain. Keep in mind, every Spanish-speaking country has some language details specific to them so it would be essential to do some research on the specific country or countries that you will visit.

I will now list some tips that I have found useful and should be very helpful to you in your journey of learning Spanish. I don't wish you luck because that will not get you anywhere- reading this book, dedicating yourself, and taking some risks will!

Important note

<u>Due to the nature of this book (it contains charts, graphs, and so on), you will better your reading experience by setting your device on *LANDSCAPE* mode!</u>

Language Tips

Tip #1 - Keep an Open Mind

It may seem obvious but you must understand that languages are very different from each other. You cannot expect them to translate word for word. '*There is a black dog*' will not translate word for word with the same word order in Spanish. You have to get used to the idea of translating WHOLE ideas. So don't find yourself saying, "*Why is everything backwards in Spanish?*" because it may seem that way many times. Keep your mind open to the many differences that you will find in the language that go far beyond just the words.

Tip #2 - Take Risks

Be fearless. Talk to as many people as you can. The more practice you get the better and don't worry about looking like a fool when you say, "*I am pregnant*" rather than "*I am embarrassed,*" which as you will find out can be a common mistake. If anyone is laughing remember they are not laughing at you. Just laugh with them, move on, and LEARN from it, which brings us to our next tip.

Tip #3 - Learn from your Mistakes

It doesn't help to get down because you made one more mistake when trying to order at a restaurant, take a taxi, or just in a friendly conversation. Making mistakes is a HUGE part of learning a language. You have to put yourself out there as we said and be willing to make tons of mistakes! Why? Because what can you do with mistakes. You can LEARN from them. If you never make a mistake, you probably are not learning as much as you could. So every time you mess up when trying to communicate, learn from it, move on, and keep your head up!

Tip #4 - Immerse yourself in the language

If you're not yet able to go to a Spanish-speaking country, try to pretend that you are. Surround yourself with Spanish. Listen to music in Spanish, watch movies, TV shows, in Spanish. Play games on your phone, computer, etc. in Spanish. Another great idea is to actually put your phone, computer, tablet and/or other electronic devices in Spanish. It can be frustrating at first but in the end this exposure will definitely pay off.

Tip #5 - Start Thinking in Spanish

I remember being a senior in high school and working as a lifeguard at a fairly deserted pool. While I was sitting and staring at the empty waters, I would speak to myself or think to myself (to not seem so crazy) in Spanish. I would describe my surroundings, talk about what I had done and what I was going to do, etc. While I was riding my bike, I would do the same thing. During any activity when you don't need to talk or think about anything else, keep your brain constantly going in Spanish to get even more practice in the language. So get ready to turn off the English and jumpstart your Spanish brain!

Tip #6 - Label your Surroundings/Use Flashcards

When I started to learn Portuguese, I bought an excellent book that included stickers so that you could label your surroundings. So I had stickers all over my parents' house from the kitchen to the bathroom that labeled the door, the dishes, furniture, parts of the house, etc. It was a great, constant reminder of how to say these objects in another language. You can just make your own labels and stick them all over the house and hope it doesn't bother your family or housemates too much!

Tip #7 - Use Context clues, visuals, gestures, expressions, etc.

If you don't understand a word that you have heard or read, look or listen to the surrounding words and the situation to help you. If you are in a restaurant and your friend says, "I am going to ??? a sandwich." You can take a guess that she said *order* or *eat* but you don't have to understand every word in order to understand the general meaning. When you are in a conversation use gestures, expressions, and things around you to help communicate your meaning. Teaching English as a second language to young learners taught me this. If you act everything out, you are more likely to get your point across. If you need to say the word *bird* and you don't know how you can start flapping your arms and chirping and then you will get your point across and possibly learn how to say *bird*. It may seem ridiculous but as I said, you have to be willing to look silly to learn another language and this greatly helps your language communication and learning.

Tip #8 - Circumlocution

Circumlo... what? This is just a fancy word for describing something when you don't know how to say it. If you are looking to buy an umbrella and don't know how to say it, what can you do? You can describe it using words you know. You can say, it is something used for the rain that opens and closes and then hopefully someone will understand you, help you, and maybe teach you how to say this word. Using circumlocution is excellent language practice and is much better than just giving up when you don't know how to say a word. So keep talking even if you have a limited vocabulary. Say what you can and describe or act out what you can't!

SECTION 1: THE BASICS

Chapter 1: Getting the Pronunciation Down

Below I will break down general Spanish pronunciation for the whole alphabet dividing it into vowels and consonants. One great thing about Spanish is that the letters almost always stay consistent as far as what sound they make. Unlike English in which the vowels can make up to 27 different sounds depending on how they are mixed. Be thankful that you don't have to learn English or at least have already learned English. There are of course some sounds in Spanish that we never make in English and you possibly have never made in your life. So get ready to start moving your mouth and tongue in a new way that may seem strange at first but as I keep saying, practice makes perfect!

The charts on the next page will explain how to say the letter, pronounce it, and if there is an example in an English word of how to say it I put it in the right column.

Vowel Sounds

Vowel	How to say the letter	How to pronounce it in a word	As in...
a	Ah	Ah	T<u>a</u>co
e	Eh	Eh	<u>E</u>gg
i	Ee	Ee	<u>Easy</u>
o	Oh	Oh	<u>O</u>pen
u	Oo	Oo	B<u>oo</u>k

Consonant Sounds

Consonant	How to say the letter	How to pronounce it in a word	As in...
b	beh	similar to English b	
c	ceh	k after *a, o,* or *u* s after *e* or *i*	cat cereal
ch	cheh	ch	cheese
d	deh	a soft d (place your tongue at the back of your upper teeth)	three
f	efe	F	free
g	geh	h before i or e g before a, o, u	him go
h	ache	silent	
j	hota	H	him
k	kah	K	karaoke
l	ele	like English l with tongue raised to roof of mouth	
ll	eye	Y	yes
m	eme	M	money
n	ene	N	no
ñ	enye	Ny	canyon
p	peh	like English p but you don't aspirate	

Consonants continued

Consonant	How to say the letter	How to pronounce it in a word	As in...
Q	koo	k (q is always followed by u like English)	quilt
R	ere	* at the beginning of a word you	

		must roll your r's by vibrating tongue at roof of mouth * in the middle of a word it sounds like a soft d	
rr	<u>erre</u>	roll your r's as mentioned above	
S	<u>ese</u>	Like English s	<u>s</u>orry
T	<u>teh</u>	a soft English t, the tongue touches the back of the upper teeth	
V	<u>veh</u>	like Spanish b	<u>b</u>oots

Consonants continued

Consonant	How to say the letter	How to pronounce it in a word	As in…
w	<u>dobleveh</u>	like English w	<u>w</u>ater
x	<u>equis</u>	*Between vowels and at the end of a word, it sounds like the English *ks*. *At the beginning of a word, it sounds like the letter *s*.	*bo<u>x</u> *<u>s</u>orry
y	<u>igriega</u>	like English y	<u>y</u>ellow
z	seta	s	<u>s</u>ix

Note: If you're not sure how to pronounce a word, one thing you can do is type it in *Google translate* then click on the little speaker icon in the bottom left corner to hear the correct pronunciation.

<u>To check out the rest of "Learn Spanish In 7 DAYS!" Go to Amazon and Look for it Right Now!</u>

Check Out My Other Books

Are you ready to exceed your limits? Then pick a book from the one below and start learning yet another new language. I can't imagine anything more fun, fulfilling, and exciting!

If you'd like to see the entire list of language guides (there are a ton more!), go to:

>>http://www.amazon.com/Dagny-Taggart/e/B00K54K6CS/<<

About the Author

Dagny Taggart is a language enthusiast and polyglot who travels the world, inevitably picking up more and more languages along the way.

Taggart's true passion became learning languages after she realized the incredible connections with people that it fostered. Now she just can't get enough of it. Although it's taken time, she has acquired vast knowledge on the best and fastest ways to learn languages. But the truth is, she is driven simply by her motive to build exceptional links and bonds with others.

She is inspired everyday by the individuals she meets across the globe. For her, there's simply not anything as rewarding as practicing languages with others because she gets to make friends with people from all that come from a variety of cultures. This, in turn, has broadened her mind and thinking more than she would have ever imagined it could.

Of course, as a result of her constant travels, Taggart has become an expert on planning trips and making the most of time spent out of what she calls her "base" town. She jokes that she's practically at the nomad status now, but she's more content to live that way.

She knows how to live on a manageable budget weather she's in Paris or Phnom Penh. She knows how to seek out the adventures and thrills, no doubt, lying in wait at any city she visits. She knows that reflection on each every experience is significant if she wants to grow as a traveler and student of the world's cultures.

Because of this, Taggart chooses to share her understanding of languages and travel so that others, too, can experience the same life-altering benefits she has.

Made in the USA
Lexington, KY
03 February 2015